The Leader Connection

Shanda Mints

The Leader Connection

From Managing People to Leading Them

Shanda Mints

Disclaimer: The thoughts, opinions, and ideas expressed in this manuscript are entirely my own and are not intended to represent the views or beliefs of any organization, company, or individual I may be associated with, past or present.

Published by Game Changer Publishing

Paperback ISBN: 978-1-965653-70-8

Hardcover ISBN: 978-1-965653-71-5

Digital ISBN: 978-1-965653-72-2

GAME CHANGER
PUBLISHING

www.GameChangerPublishing.com

Dedication

To my teams and my readers,

Here's the starting baton.
Put your fingerprints all over it,
and then
pass it on.

Read This First

Just to say thanks for buying and reading my book, I would like to give you a few free bonus gifts, no strings attached!

Scan the QR Code Here:

The Leader Connection
From Managing People to Leading Them

Shanda Mints

GAME CHANGER PUBLISHING

www.GameChangerPublishing.com

Foreword

I have a lot to say about this book. Its strong values resonate with me, as I am sure they will resonate with others on the leadership path. The way Shanda describes the difference between a manager and a leader is spot on.

Shanda organizes her concepts in a way that's easy to follow. She writes about ideas like giving back to others, which I hope readers will see as a true gift. I found myself nodding as I read. She references both well-known figures and personal experiences, and the mixture is refreshing.

I absolutely loved the idea of recognizing and remembering those who helped you get where you are. In change management, this is essential for any project. You must celebrate the wins and conduct after-action reviews for adoption and continuous improvement. When people are recognized, and they know it, ownership kicks in. If people are recognized and they don't know it, it creates a powerful, Zen-like pause. Shanda reminds you to consider those who traveled the path before you and took care of it. She gently calls you to recognize that you didn't get here alone and that it's your job to tend to the path for those who follow.

In her book, Shanda integrates science and religion, making

space for both to coexist. In her references to religions that are not her own, she brings us into her head and reminds us how we would serve ourselves and our teams better if we checked a lot of stuff at the door. She asks us to bring our best, authentic selves and show up with this in mind when we come to our teams and meetings.

As a Change Management leader, I appreciated the references to an invention methodology, such as those of Bezos, versus the fixed culture that most companies have today. The fixed culture of living quarter to quarter breeds managers rather than leaders and makes the transition from manager to leader more difficult than it has to be. *The Leader Connection* helps bridge that gap, making the path clearer for leaders to journey down.

I hope you all enjoy the book as much as I did.

—Michelle Chiodi, Change Navigation Coach

Contents

Author's Note

This book is different.

It reads like a handbook or study guide, but it's about a journey through what it takes to grow your teams and change your leadership styles as your team scales. If you're a new manager or you've been managing for a while and now need to grow your team at scale, this book will guide you to some useful tools.

We won't cover sales and marketing funnels, which are critical to scaling your business. That's another book by another author. This study guide is focused on growing sustainable teams. The tools within will be most beneficial to knowledge workers, especially in delivery or operations roles, though I suspect that several can be applied in other environments as well. Like most study guides, this guide only has 80% of the answers, if that. Your job is to fill in the blanks with your journey.

The Leader Connection is about drawing connections between one set of ideas and applying them to similar but different situations to help you scale your team. Simply put, it's using your resources to the max. This will help you transition from manager to leader. You're going to learn some foundational tools that are important to growing your teams at scale. You'll learn why it takes something different to lead small teams and large ones. You'll hear about offshoots and discover why the principles and lessons work.

But this book is not for everyone. If you are looking for a silver bullet or want an easy button, I have news for you: you won't find it here. I'm not convinced you're going to find it anywhere. While I am giving you a set of tools that usually take years of experience to discover, they are still tools. You have to put them to use in the work ahead. However, if you're willing to do the work, you will reap the rewards.

Join me as we explore business and look at some of the principles and fundamental aspects that also show up in science, math, history, and religion. Why use science and religion in a book about growing teams? Among other things, I lead a team of analysts, and predictive analytics is all about identifying trends and applying them to similar situations.

We will explore themes that have withstood the test of time and learn how we can leverage that knowledge to help us become a better-connected leader. But don't worry if you don't have an advanced degree in science or religion. Neither do I. I don't have to go too deep to find connections, and I'll provide little refreshers along the way. We also will collect advice from some of the foremost experts on leadership as well as some of the leaders from well-known organizations.

I invite you to pick up and put down this book—it's written so you can flip through and skim the highlights or dive deep and get details beyond the details. This journey plays out most clearly in order, but like most journeys, you may not see the full picture until you come to the end and reflect on where you've been.

So, why should you trust me?

My superpower is developing teams that work and systems that are both scalable and sustainable. Many people can grow, but not many can sustain that scale. Over the past 25 years, I've grown teams from the ground up and inherited many at-risk teams. Each time, I've been able to help stabilize them. I've found that you have to constantly flip between growth mode and sustain mode, depending on the growth period of the team. I've seen all kinds of company sizes and dynamics, both from working in them and from consulting with them. I have worked at small, medium, and large organizations, and for years, I was responsible for 1,400 employees across 15 countries.

It's not enough that I have taught teams how to scale several times and taken them through the process. Building teams for other companies is what I do for a living. Along my journey of growth, I've led teams and consultants whose job it is to design, build, and scale teams for other companies. Over my career, I have worked with hundreds of clients, from small to some of the largest in the world. These clients varied in industries from healthcare to technology, and many others in between.

Please note, while I draw on my experiences, my thoughts and views are my own and should not be attributed to my employer or any of its clients. In order to avoid the risk of a confidentiality breach, I deliberately left out clients I've worked with. Any mention of specific companies in this book is based on my research and publicly available information.

Beyond all that, I have another superpower: seeing connections and what it takes to make changes. I've led several different kinds of teams. I've led tech teams and helped build a proprietary technology, which we sold to our clients 15 years before similar products became popular. I've led data analysts, whose job it is to take data elements and relate them to business outcomes. I've built new delivery centers and call centers from the ground up in countries where we didn't have an entity previously. I've led teams of administrators, teams of recruiters, and advertising teams. I also lead a team of project managers who live in project plans and change management techniques. I am uniquely positioned for this book because I've had the advantage of scanning across functions, industries, and even countries to see which leadership themes work at both small and large scales.

That's me in business. However, like my readers, I'm so much more than the hats I wear for work. I've always been fascinated with religion and learning. I even wrote my graduate thesis on the impact of various translations of Bible text, going into the original Greek and Hebrew interlinear versions to read the original wording. From there, I was hooked on going back to original sources to gain a new perspective. After 9/11, even though I'm very strong in my Christian beliefs, I did a self-study on Islam to make sure I didn't grow hate due to the actions of a few extremists. This deep dive was the beginning of my studies into other religions, such as Buddhism and Hinduism, all the while relating the teachings to my Christian roots.

Why science? My grandfather, who raised me, was a brilliant programmer and mathematician who worked for the military as a civilian consultant even after he left the Army. While working with the inventor Gordon Matthews, my grandfather was one of the four founding brains behind voicemail, one of the early explorers to convert speech to zeros and ones and then back to speech. He engineered the first voicemail message exchange system. I remember reams of paper filled with nothing but zeros and ones that my grandfather could read in a way most of us read a book. He was a learner for life and had a passion for science and sci-fi.

As my grandfather aged and programming languages changed, he moved away from programming and deeper into studies of quantum physics. He wasn't a natural socializer, and he lacked the knack for small talk, especially not with a young woman like me. So, as a young adult, I researched quantum physics on the side just so we could have engaging conversations. I am not a scientist by training; I am just a girl trying to keep up with conversations with her beloved grandfather.

One day, I saw it—the connections between science, math, religion, and business. I'm not always right when I try to connect things, but I use my resources for validation. I'm well connected, too, and I lean in on others for expertise. All. The. Time.

Just as each of our lives is different, this book is different.

Science is built on laws and theories that describe how the universe works. They can be used as predictive indicators in unexplored situations. Both laws and theories are accurate and accepted until new evidence proves otherwise. Finding new evidence is a lightbulb "aha" moment that leads to the discovery of new principles. The tools in this book are listed as "Ahas," indicating a discovery that a broader principle might be at play.

Aha moments are everywhere. In science, they hint at principles, and principles lead to laws. They aren't the law themselves because some principles change shape under different environments, but a consistent principle, regardless of the circumstance, indicates that a law might be at play. The principle is the truth behind the laws that govern our natural world.

At our core, we are all little versions of our universe. The atoms in our body are little mirrors of the solar systems above. They function because of scientific laws. We may not understand all these laws and the various dynamics at play acting on our systems, but the more we study behaviors and outcomes, the closer we get. As a connected leader, understanding this concept is like shining a flashlight into what's ahead and seeing what's there before you arrive.

Isn't leading just going in a particular direction first? To lead, you've got to be a bit of a freelancer, doing something that no one else has done before anyone else even knows it's something to do. The leader is the first to go in that direction, and that part of the news is difficult for some people. Being first in the journey can be intimidating if you don't know where you're going or what tools to bring. So, let's pick up some tools together. Going to new places is hard enough, but going there without tools to help you navigate the new territory is like being in the dark without a flashlight.

Pack your flashlight, a swimsuit, a net, and a parachute.

We're going on an adventure.

then, I'm only reaping the benefits of my experiences and sharing them. I'm a copycat, but I'm not ashamed of it. I'm simply aware of it.

> *It's like genetics. You can take DNA from two people to make a third unique person. I enjoy taking the lessons others have learned and picking and choosing my favorite, thus making a brand that is uniquely me.*
>
> *Many scientific theories are created the same way. They take two or more other theories to come up with a new one. For instance, the theory of relativity is made up of special relativity, where we get the space-time continuum, and general relativity, which refines Newton's law of universal gravitation. Atomic theory uses chemistry, physics, and mathematics. Even the theory of evolution evolved from multiple theories, using principles from genetics, paleontology, and ecology to explain diversity.*

I hope you've already come to recognize that we are all products of the people, books, and experiences that have impacted us. You are unique, but you are not the product of your uniqueness. You're the product of other people's uniqueness, and other people will be the product of your uniqueness. We are irrevocably interconnected.

When you think about it, there's an enormous responsibility to seize the opportunity to learn and share our learning. Each moment calls us to be fully present so that we may interact with people, places, feelings, or things around us in such a way as to bring the best possible next moment forward, which will ignite the next moment in an infinite series of moments to follow.

We're called to be catalysts for each moment, but there's no need to stress about this calling. It's not a burden but a blessing. You're called to be exactly who you are. Who you have been to this point is exactly who you needed to be to get here, but it's not who you will need to be to get forward. I hope that in the pages to come, you'll

Chapter 1
Connections

"Even so, the body is not made up of one part but many."
–I Corinthians 12:14 (NIV)

One summer morning, I went to our local swimming pool, excited about jumping off the high dive for the first time. You see, only days before, I had mastered the art of the cannonball off the low diving board, and I'd been too chicken to try it off the high one. But not today. Today, I was determined to take the plunge. So, I packed up my towel, put on my one-piece and flip-flops, and helped my sister get her floaties in our bag, and we went off with my aunt to the public pool down the street.

I couldn't believe our luck when we arrived: three decent lounge chairs sitting right by the diving boards were still available. My aunt would have the perfect view of my amazing feat. The only problem is that sitting right next to the chairs were some school girls maybe a year older than me. These were not just any fifth graders. They were the sunbathing, mature fifth graders with the cute little two-pieces and sunglasses who were likely doing swan dives off the high board and certainly not doing cannonballs.

Not letting this deter me, I took off my sun hat, revealing my white head of hair. As soon as I took off my coverup, revealing my swimsuit and bare skin, I heard one of the girls say, "Look at her. I've never seen someone so pale. What's wrong with her?" She started laughing and pointed at me.

Now, this was back in the '80s in the United States. Back then, being pale was not a symbol of taking care of yourself. It was a mark of uncoolness. Standing there, I had never felt so uncool in my life. Suddenly, my white hair, which had been my golden crown, was stringy and blinding. My skin was nearly translucent. My one-piece suit was hot pink with flowers and screamed of childish daydreams. My flip-flops were plastic, my towel tattered.

As I held back tears, I could see everything about me turn uncool, everything I hadn't even questioned minutes before. I grabbed my sister by the arm and told her we were leaving. She started whining and complaining, but I was set on getting out of there. My aunt graciously appeased me, and we ducked out, never to jump from the high rise, never to even make it off the ground.

In work, as in life, there are many times when you think that you have it all pulled together. There are times when you've set yourself up to succeed and set your mind to achieve your goals, and then something unexpected happens to land you flat on your butt, making you question your very core. Has this ever happened to you? If you're like most of us, it has.

So, here are a few questions: How do you get the courage to rise up again when the external world seems to be laughing at you and wanting to keep you from getting off the ground? How do you get the courage to stay in the uncomfortable moments when everything seems to be going against you, and one thing after another seems to be going wrong all at once?

If my fourth-grade self had paired the vision of jumping off the high dive with the foundation of knowing who I was and that I was wonderfully made, I might have had the wisdom to ignore the external naysayers and stick with my plan. But the fact is, the plan was already scary to me, and my self-image was already paper-thin.

So, when the external factors reinforced my fears, I cracked under pressure and abandoned my plan.

This same experience happens frequently as we're scaling our teams. Often, the thing that we're most afraid of but often don't take the time to address at the core is the thing that distracts us from our goals and achieving the potential within us.

I was an awkward child, and I thought my uniqueness made me awkward. But later, I realized my uniqueness made me special, and my negative thoughts about my uniqueness made me awkward. When I embraced my differences and learned how they could benefit others, I became so much stronger, and others wanted to be around me. This shy, awkward, uncertain child grew into a strong, confident, enthusiastic leader who could help other leaders gain fundamental skills that would enable them to grow and scale their teams.

How did I do it? First, I had to focus on myself. As a young manager, I was not a strong one, but like so many other first-time managers, I was an effective individual contributor. As a new manager, I'd either tell people to do it like I did it, or I would do it for them. It was exhausting! I was doing my job and theirs. Whenever I talked to my manager about being overloaded, I got the typical response: "Work smarter, not harder."

What does that even mean? Of course, I was working as smartly as I could. I was leaning into technology as much as possible. I could run circles around others on efficiency and when it came to doing projects the fastest way. So, when my boss said to work smarter and not harder, it was like they were sweeping my concerns under the rug. They didn't show me what that meant, so I had to take matters into my own hands and figure it out for myself.

And I did.

At least, I figured it out, but it wasn't by myself.

Let me tell you a secret about managers that you may not know. The good ones cheat.

They don't intend to cheat, but they have a clear advantage that people on the front lines don't often realize. Are you for one of my earliest Aha moments, one that led to a multiplier later on?

Connections

Aha #1: Managers learn from their direct reports.

Once you do something, it's a lot easier to do it again. If you have direct reports, you don't have to be the doer; you can be the observer. Let's say a direct report climbs a daunting mountain and gives you feedback on how they did it. Once you see it done, it's easier to do it yourself. In a different situation, if you have seen an employee go down the wrong path, you can identify it earlier when someone else ventures down that same path. Line staff usually only see the results of someone else's work, but managers see the journey from the outside and can learn from the situations and reactions of their employees.

Let's take our first journey to science while we get ready to pack our toolkit. Why does Aha #1 work?

Einstein's theory of relativity states that everything is relative to your perspective. The theory of relativity itself is a combination of two theories: special relativity and general relativity. Let's start with special relativity. In a vacuum, the speed of light is constant no matter where you monitor it. However, Einstein found that if you monitor it from different perspectives, it looks different to you. It's not just light that does this. Other things, like sound, do, too (the Doppler effect). General Relativity states that light bends due to gravity, and it allows us to predict the existence of massive objects based on the curvature of light.

We won't go deeper into science than this because these simple definitions give us enough insight to draw connections between this phenomenon and human behavior in business. Let's play out these three concepts of relativity:

1. Speed is relative to your perspective.

2. Gravitational pull bends light.

3. You can use that knowledge to predict large objects.

Now let's draw some connections to human behavior. Instead of "speed of light," let's put something else there—in this case, let's use "difficulty of a challenge."

    1. Difficulty is relative to your perspective.

    2. The complexity of the challenge impacts the perception of the difficulty.

    3. You can predict difficulty by previous experiences.

Here's how that plays out when you connect the concepts: Earning a million dollars may seem insurmountable to you unless you've done it several times already. For someone who's already a millionaire, it doesn't seem so hard. Previous complexities and unknowns are more clear. You can predict what's going to happen based on your past experiences.

My team members bring me problems and challenges all the time. Sometimes, they solve them on their own, and sometimes, they need my help. However, most of the time, it is easier for me to see the solution than it is for them simply because I am removed from the situation and have the advantage of perspective.

Imagine a picture where, when zoomed in, you can't tell what's going on because you're too close to it.

By being removed from the situation, I could more clearly see the things that they were too close to see. I had perspective on my side.

By watching the experiences of others, you will identify their blind spots. If you apply the theory of relativity and are willing to accept their blind spots as something repeatable in similar situations, you can then apply their learnings and sound super smart to your other employees by guiding them before they ever get to the experience.

Aha #1 is powerful, but there's a multiplier to the advantage of having a different perspective from your direct reports, and that's Aha #2.

Aha #2: Believe for yourself as others have taught you.

To move from Aha #1 to Aha #2, use the mirror test. Here's how it works: Take the lessons of others and hold up a mirror to yourself to see if you can see their situation in your own leadership. The magic of this test is that when you uncover a blind spot, you can address it before anyone else points it out to you. Managers have the advantage of the mirror test, something first-line employees don't.

The Leader Connection

I found that if I were being honest with myself, 99% of the issues people brought to me were issues that I could relate to. Either I had experienced them in the past, or I was experiencing them now. Having my team bring me the issue was a gift of perspective in my management journey. If I could apply everything somebody brought to me as a learning journey on my own, I could exponentially get better. I wasn't just learning from my mistakes but from the mistakes of those around me. You've got to be willing to learn from your mistakes. It's a principle of growth. If something is preventing you from growing, you have to correct it before replicating it, or you will replicate damaged products.

When you accept others' blind spots as your own and are willing to learn from them, you can leverage their learnings as your own and gain speed and momentum on your journey to improvement. That's why this is a multiplier for scale. You don't have to experience everything yourself. You can use what others have learned and apply it to your situations without going through the process of trial and error.

What a huge advantage people managers have! Where else can you see your issues and solutions multiplied?

- You have to be willing to accept that you don't know everything.
- You have to be willing to let another's mistake be your own —really internalize it.
- You have to be willing to learn from your mistakes.

If you're willing to do these things, you can speed up your learning.

Good people managers have the luxury of perspective. They can see what others are dealing with and help them get through their problems. They can also remove their own obstacles. Many of the lessons from my years of managing others were learned *because* I was managing others.

learn how to be the person you're called to be. But first, some of you may need a little help seeing the person you are now.

Think about something you're very proud of. Maybe you raised amazing children. Maybe you're a fantastic soccer player. Maybe you did something brilliant at work. Maybe you're a great cook. Maybe you helped someone out of a bind. Maybe you've even published a book or started a flourishing business. Maybe, just maybe, you're proud of the fact that you've chosen to get out of bed today.

All of these things are wonderful, but not a single one was achieved without many, many people influencing you. Some gave you the tools to succeed. Maybe it was a parent, a coach, a mentor. Others, by simply being horrible examples, showed you what not to do. If you're being honest with yourself, you may be able to see that nothing you've done was yours alone.

Now, if you're able to accept that fact, hopefully, you will be called to temper your pride. At the very least, you'll recognize that your hard work was the product of other people investing in you. And when you're praised, you'll appreciate that praise for what it truly is: recognition of the amazing people, books, feelings, and experiences you've responded to. Instead of letting the praise flow to you, start to let it flow through you to the others who have helped you achieve what you have.

This is the leader connection:

What Was Given to You + Your Lens = Your Ahas
Your Ahas, Given to Others = Your Legacy

Legacy builders pass on what they have. The connected leader uses what was given to them from all their resources and then makes it their own to pass on to those who will come after them. I'm not afraid to use all my resources. The people I meet teach me things. Whether it be an excellent boss or a bad one, I learn from them. I learn from books, people, classes, and experiences. I learn from science, religion, and art. And what I've learned, I'm storing into resources to pull from when I need to. Nelson Mandela, the first Black president of South Africa and known for ending racial segregation in his country, once said, "I never lose. I either win or learn." It's not the experiences alone that make us better people; it's how we respond to those experiences that determines our trajectory.

So, what does a connected leader look like? The first couple of chapters in this book provide the answer.

Chapter 2 will take us through a well-connected leader's qualities:

- Qualities that lead to **PERSPECTIVE**
    - Curious
    - Humble
    - Empathetic
- Qualities that lead to **CONNECTION**
    - Honest
    - Inspirational
    - Gracious
    - Merciful
- Qualities that lead to **APPLICATION**
    - Resilient
    - Motivated
    - Creative
    - Resourceful

Chapter 3 will walk us through what a well-connected leader understands:

- The power of the vision
- The importance of position and the pointed right model
- Management fundamentals

We'll take a quick detour in **Chapter 4** to discuss the fuel that powers the team before we start the engine.

Chapter 5 walks us through how a well-connected leader executes effectively.

While the first five chapters are about setting the foundation for any team size, **Chapters 6–10** are about doing it at scale.

Now that you know what a well-connected leader looks like, you can push through those challenges with your new leader hat and create brilliant, scalable teams. Easy, right? If it were so easy, we'd have more teams succeeding than failing. Nothing I've said about the qualities of a leader, what they understand, and what they do hasn't already been said many times before. That's exactly my point. These are themes that come up time and time again. I didn't create them; I just called out some of the patterns. So, why is this so hard to do?

It's not that they're hard; it's that they aren't always the obvious choice at the moment. Sometimes, the world focuses on what it takes to get ahead in terms of negative behaviors like greed, backstabbing, cutthroat competition, and taking advantage of others. Many people have great distrust for leaders, and with good reason. It's gotten so bad that many have stopped wanting to be a leader because they don't want to be associated with "the man" and all the work and negativity associated with the title.

Well, I have great news.

Aha #4: Things change.

This is so agreed upon that maybe it's more than an Aha. It's at least a principle, if not a law. It's been observed for thousands of years. Heraclitus, a renowned Greek philosopher who lived around 540 BCE, famously stated, "The only constant in life is change."

The great leaders of today won't be the great leaders of tomorrow. The businesses that are on top today may not even exist 25 years from now. Things change, but laws remain constant, and principles are built on the laws of the universe. Wouldn't it be great to know some of the basic principles that withstand the test of time?

I don't pretend to make your journey an easy one. In fact, that would be dumb because one of the principles is that the journey is challenging, and through the challenge, we grow. From here on out, reframe your thinking. You're not going through a problem; you're growing through a problem.

If you're thinking your problems are, well, problems, then we need to reframe that, too. They are difficulties you're facing. They may be barriers right now, but they're not problems blocking you. They are challenges for you to grow through.

When you make the simple move from the word "problem" to the word "challenge," all of a sudden, the situation is no longer a show-stopper but a fun game to navigate through, where growth is as much of a reward as the solution is.

Now you have a challenge ahead. Whatever your challenge is today, it is not your real challenge. Your real challenge is seeing how what you learn from today's experiences can be applied to future challenges so that you can grow through those challenges more quickly.

Aha #5: Applying today's learnings to tomorrow's challenges improves efficiency.

If you're constantly growing through challenges, you're building resiliency and capacity for energy so that when the next challenge arises, you're ready to overcome it with greater force than you did in prior challenges.

The science this draws from is the law of the conservation of energy, which says that energy can neither be created nor destroyed. It can, however, be transformed. All energy that exists within the universe exists right now. The forms of the energy change, however.

Now, let's see how this changes within an open system. The first law of thermodynamics states that as energy moves through a system, the system's internal energy rises or falls depending on the energy that has come or gone. When we meet with external factors, the energy of those forces can be transferred to the original force. Now that you have had that little science refresher, go back and read Aha #5 again with a new perspective. Your past challenges and learnings give you energy for your future challenges.

Aha #6: The challenge is energizing.

When you change your perspective, the challenge has a form of energy that's ready for the taking. Whenever I feel like a challenge is causing me great angst, I don't want to face it. The burden of not wanting it makes it harder to navigate. Whenever I am capable of stepping outside of the challenge and looking at what I can learn from it, the sheer act of changing my perspective makes the challenge easier to navigate. Nothing has changed about the challenge except my perspective.

As you grow through a challenge and learn new ways to overcome it, you gain energy that can be used in the next challenge that awaits. While this concept can be extremely energizing, it requires an active shift in perspective or else the challenge becomes exhausting. The key is the shift in perspective. Challenges today give us the knowledge we need to overcome challenges in the future. We grow through challenges. When we see the exact same challenge, the growth we've gained the last time makes the new challenge less daunting.

Imagine coming to a fork in the road on your journey. You see a sign that says *"easy path"* with an arrow pointing one way and *"hard path"* with an arrow pointing the other, and you know that at the end of each path, there's a treasure. Which path do you take? The easy path, right? Okay, now imagine that at the end of the easy path, before you get to the treasure, there's a cave. The entrance to the cave is blocked by a boulder that cannot be moved unless you have picked up tools along the way. There's no possible way to remove the boulder without the tools, and the only path that has the tools is the hard one. Now the hard path is not looking so bad, is it? That's what I meant when I said, "The challenge itself has a form of energy that's ready for the taking." It creates opportunities for you to pick up new tools.

Sometimes, when life seems overwhelming, the best course of action is to pause and step outside of the situation to gain perspective. Hopefully, at this point, you see a need to move differently than before. So, where do we start?

In his book, *The 7 Habits of Highly Effective People*, Stephen R. Covey, a renowned author, educator, and business consultant, says, "Begin with the end in mind." This emphasizes the importance of having a clear vision of your goals and desired outcomes before starting a project. Connect this! On any journey, begin with the end in mind.

Some of you might ask, "Can't I just get started and see where the path takes me?"

Yes, absolutely!

If you're interested in exploring what might be out there, you don't have to know the exact coordinates of your destination point. One of the best trips of my life was when my college friends and I backpacked through Western Europe for a month. We had a general idea of what cities we were going to be in on what days, but we didn't pre-plan everything that we would be doing. We got there and had to figure it out along the way.

But that was the end goal, wasn't it? It wasn't seeing the Louvre in France or the (Leaning) Tower of Pisa in Italy. The goal was the journey.

In business, saying, "The goal is the journey," doesn't translate into an effective ROI, at least not in any for-profit business I've experienced. The goal in most businesses is to make a profit, and to begin with that end in mind, you need to have some idea of how you are going to achieve that objective.

Aha #7: Your foundation sets you up for your future.

So, what do you need to add to your toolkit now that will help you later on?

When looking at the leaders, both now and in the past, it's helpful to ask these questions: What qualities do they have that help them succeed? What do they understand? What do they do that we can model as leaders? Do any of these themes go deeper than principles? Are any of these themes built on the very laws of nature? If so, those are the ones I want to emulate. Can I use them to my advantage to gain momentum from the flow that's already created? I believe that you can, but there's a risk here. If you don't set the right foundation, you can end up doing significant damage along the way.

Getting the foundation right is critical to building a house that can withstand the test of time. I'm reminded of the fable of the three pigs. The first was quite lazy, and his house collapsed first. The second was slightly smarter, though still lazy, and his house also crumbled. It was only the third pig, who worked his tail off, pun intended, through sweat and tears and did the heavy lifting that was able to build a house, who not only survived the wolf's attack but also sheltered his brothers, who had wasted away their opportunities.

Aha #8: Scale is about layers.

You can't scale without adding layers upon layers of reinforcement. And if your layers are founded on the wrong principles, the final product will be all wrong.

If I wanted to bake a lasagna but used lesser-quality ingredients, then my lasagna would taste bad. The first person to try it might eat a whole piece, to be polite, but they're not going to come back for seconds. Now, imagine if I were to use cardboard instead of pasta. Of course, I could still bake a lasagna and call it lasagna, but upon cutting into it, the unsuspecting victim would, at best, laugh. So, what are the ingredients for the foundation and layers of reinforcement? You likely already know from looking at your own managers.

Future connection moment: We've created some worksheets for the exercises in this book and put them on www.MintROI.com so you can keep them together. We will be designing the vision and organizational structure for your organization, and you might want to keep them all together. You don't have to use the work-sheets if you don't want to; a journal or piece of paper works just fine. For those who are interested, there are two bonus exercises at www.MintROI.com.

Have you ever played this common new manager exercise?

1. Think of a leader you don't like. What qualities do they have that you don't like?
2. Now, don't do those.
3. Think of a leader you do like. What qualities do they have that you like about them?
4. Do more of those.

I've done this exercise myself many times, each time thinking of managers I enjoyed working with and also of managers I didn't enjoy as much. I began doing more of those things that I liked and fewer of the ones I didn't. Eventually, I realized that my team might one day think of me as one of the strong or weak managers. Would I be in the group of the ones they liked or the ones they didn't like? This helped me elevate my quest of selecting more positive and less negative behaviors.

I suspect most of us agree that a leader and a people manager are different. At the core, a manager is responsible for the day-to-day work of others, whereas a leader is responsible for setting the direction for a group of people. A manager can be a leader. A leader can be a manager. Not all managers are leaders, and not all leaders are managers. You will have informal leaders on your team who don't manage people. But if you are responsible for growing a team, chances are you are both a manager and a leader. For this book, I am talking about people who are both.

Please give me some grace when I flip between these two hats that the person may need to wear. There are many books on management theory and leadership. This book uses interdisciplinary connections to explain the why behind the what. It's about the business themes that arise time and time again, whether through math, science, or ancient philosophical and religious teachings.

Aha #3: Leadership is not easy.

Pick your pain. Pay now or pay later. Life's not easy, but it's not hard, either. Some ways are more or less difficult than others, but if I've learned something in life, if something is easy now, you're only delaying the hard. And if it's hard now, it's going to get easier later. Delayed gratification usually pays off more in the end than the immediate reward. I've learned that if I choose the path of delayed gratification and, at the same time, change my interim objective to the journey as the reward, I'm doubly blessed. I learned this by watching others. There's always that person who seems happy no matter what road they are on. To me, that's the real win. So, I adapt my mindset while gearing up for the long haul.

Among other things, I'm a phenomenal copycat. Nothing I'm going to say or do is new. At best, I might present it in a new order, giving your mind a perspective that it has not yet experienced. Even

Maybe you don't care what your team thinks. I've heard many managers say something like, "It doesn't matter what they think. I'm the boss." An important aspect of leadership is doing the right thing regardless of whether or not it's popular. But watch me now. I said, "Doing the right thing." I didn't say, "Doing whatever you like." Very few things irk me more than a manager who says employees should listen because he said so but doesn't care what they think about it.

Have you ever heard the line, "It's not personal; it's business?" That was popular at one time, but we are past that time now. How's the tenure on their team going? How's their employment brand on Glassdoor? How much longer do you think they'll be able to sustain their team with this attitude?

Exercise 1: Begin with the end in mind

This exercise helps you see where you want to go and what you will need to do to get there.

1. What does your organization do? What would you like it to do?
2. What will it look like in one year?
3. What about five years?
4. What will you be doing in five years as a leader within this organization? What will be your role? What excites you about that role? Is it the size or the capability of the team?
5. What team members would you have around you, supporting you? Be specific. If you know the people now, name them. If you know people who represent what you would like to have, name them and the qualities they have that you like.
6. Now, how do you go about achieving that vision? If you don't know how just yet, that's ok.
   a. What are some big-ticket items you will need to be able to do?

    b. For each of the big-ticket items, what's the very next step you need to do to get started?

7. What are some obstacles in your way?
8. Who can help you remove those obstacles?
9. What financial investments will you need to make? How can you gather those finances?
10. What people investments will you need to make?
    a. Who on your team is best suited to grow to the next level?
    b. If you are doing the next level of leadership, who on your team is best prepared to do your role?
    c. What gaps does your successor have?
    d. How do you go about filling in those gaps?
    e. Take your answers from #10 to create a tentative development plan for your successor and begin working on that plan while you're still in the role you are developing them for.

Summary: Whether you prefer the analogy of collecting tools on a journey or building a house by starting with the foundation and then the frame and reinforcing it, the end result is the same. Scaling is by design and takes layers of knowledge. Leaders have faced the challenges of scaling for centuries. When we look at ancient wisdom, we can learn from the past and fast-track our knowledge towards building teams that are sustainable at scale.

Chapter 2
A Well-Connected Leader's Qualities

"To be good, and to do good, is all we have to do."
– John Adams

As eleven of us sat evenly spaced around the oval chestnut-brown table, introducing ourselves, I anxiously awaited my turn, reviewing my elevator pitch in my head over and over again. Each person was saying their name, their role, and how long they'd been with the company.

I was rehearsing these things in my head when a man four seats down took his turn and said, "I'm Brandt Hamby, and I don't really know what I do here. Mostly, I'm a janitor." Everyone laughed, and it put the whole room at ease. He had taken something that was really stuffy and made it personal and real. You see, Brandt was the COO. With his introduction, he changed the dynamic in the room, broke down the barriers, and told people he was willing to roll up his sleeves and do whatever it took. It was liquid gold.

In that moment, Brandt displayed his humor, personality, and humility, and he earned many fans. Brandt understood what was really happening in the room, the story behind the story. He knew it was far more important for our prospects to see the human side of who we were and how dedicated we were than to hear some rehearsed pitch. He connected the dots between where he was, in this case, meeting new people, and what outcome he wanted to achieve, which, in this case, was making trusted friends.

You see, trusted friends depend on one another and support each other. When you're in sales, which was one of the many hats Brandt wore, you know that someone is more likely to buy your product if they trust you.

In his intro, Brandt displayed the qualities of perspective, connection, and application. Perspective leads to belief, which leads to action. Watch this now: What you perceive is your seeing. What you believe is your being. Your actions are your doing. See. Be. Do.

What qualities give us the best perspective, which then leads to the right mindset, which then leads to the best actions? The best actions provide the most optimal outcomes.

Your position is everything. You need to get pointed in the right direction. By positioning ourselves properly, we're creating our potential, and through our potential, we're setting ourselves up for the best chances of success.

Aha #9: See good. Be good. Do good.

The phrase "Be good. Do good. See Good" is often attributed to Swami Vivekananda, a prominent Indian Hindu philosopher. It's also attributed to various movements and spiritual teachings. The Buddhists have the Eightfold Path, where putting yourself right in all your states (right belief, right speech, right mindfulness, etc.) helps you achieve happiness. In Christianity, in Philippians 4:8–9, St. Paul suggests you think about whatever is true, noble, right, etc. In all these spiritual teachings, the idea is about putting yourself in the right position first, which leads you to the right perspective (see), which then opens up your mind for the right thoughts (be), which then helps you form the right behaviors (do). This is why I've changed the order to "See Good. Be Good. Do Good."

It can be that easy, but life often makes things harder than they seem. Let's break this down below.

A Well-Connected Leader's Qualities

- Qualities that lead to **PERSPECTIVE (see)**
  - Curious
  - Humble
  - Empathetic
- Qualities that lead to **CONNECTION (be)**
  - Honest
  - Inspirational
  - Gracious
  - Merciful

- Qualities that lead to **APPLICATION (do)**
- Resilient
- Motivated
- Creative
- Resourceful

Qualities That Lead to PERSPECTIVE

When we're connecting the dots, we have to start with the dots. To see the dots, a well-connected leader must first look for them. No doubt, this sounds abundantly obvious to you, but in reality, many people who want to be leaders think they know what it takes without looking. To see good, you have to be in the right spot. This is the right position, which sets you up for the right perspective.

The Greek philosopher Socrates taught us to question everything. He gave us a way to logic and reasoning, i.e., the Socratic method. When we take this into science, we can see that the scientific method has some deep connections to logic and reasoning: identify a problem, create a hypothesis, and test it until you can come up with a conclusion. This is what perspective does for us. It allows us to see things from different angles, expanding our vision of the world.

Connected leader, listen up! We see "perspective" as an ingredient for success in both science and religion, so this is worth some pause and consideration. Matthew 6:22–23 states, "The eye is the lamp of the body. So, if your eye is healthy, your whole body will be full of light, but if your eye is bad, your whole body will be full of darkness. If then the light in you is darkness, how great is that darkness!"

In Buddhism, the Noble Eightfold Path has three paths to ensuring the right perspective. "Right belief" is about how you view life. "Right mindfulness" is about how you think about things. "Right meditation" is about discovering all the driving factors for your perspective.

Our understanding of science is all about perspective. The world was scientifically flat until it was not. The law of universal gravitation states that all objects attract each other. But then dark matter was discovered, which seems to have its own laws of gravity.

Psychology currently tells us to be aware of the stories we tell ourselves. Many of these stories have beliefs or concepts that, when left unchecked, limit our potential. The stories we tell ourselves are more real than real and truer than true—to us.

This is key: to us. It may not be real or true, but if that's our perspec-tive, then that's our truth. To give yourself the best chance of having the broadest perspective possible, you need to seek out qualities that lead to such a perspective.

A good leader will question whether they are good. To get that answer, they will want to know what good looks like. They won't just assume they know. Therefore, the logical conclusion is that a good leader is both curious and humble: humble enough to know that they may not already know the answer or, better yet, to know that they could be wrong in what they think because of their limited perspective and curious enough to want to fill in the gaps. Most people who can lead expansion initiatives are curious about what's beyond their borders. They're interested in learning more.

Curious

Samantha wasn't the best at finishing her tasks on time, but whenever there was a difficult task to be addressed, her boss would always give it to her.

When Samantha first got into a task, she would meet the various stakeholders and ask questions to understand what the current state was. She was sure to ask people separately so she could get different perspectives. Then she would ask people how they would solve the issue.

She wouldn't stop with the end users. She would reach out to the engineering teams to understand how systems work. She'd search various competitors and technologies to see how others were solving the problems.

Samantha was insatiably curious. Curiosity is a quality that separates okay work from great work. A curious person will not be okay doing what they are told just because they're told to do it. They want to understand why the thing needs to be done: why this way or that way? Because they are intent on understanding the why, they're more thorough in their output, and their output often solves the true issue.

In his influential book *Start with Why*, leadership expert Simon Sinek explores the fundamental principles of leadership and motivation. Sinek argues that to truly inspire and engage people, start with helping people understand *why* you are asking them to do something. He suggests that we need to start with inside-out leadership instead of outside-in leadership. Often, leaders explain the what, and maybe they even explain the how, but they don't usually get to the "why" or the center of the circle. He suggests that you start with the center, the "why," then get to the "how," and finally, the "what."

Sinek argues that people don't just buy products or services; they buy purpose. This is what makes the "why" so powerful. But how can you convey the why if you don't know it yourself? In the example above, Samantha understood the concept of why as the root of the purpose, and whenever she needed anything, she got it. She was so well-researched that people couldn't argue with her logic.

Learn to love learning. By learning, we grow. If we don't grow, we can't scale. If you want to work a little more on this quality, ask your team members one simple question: "Why?" Before jumping to a conclusion, ask why. Before responding to a request, ask why. Before agreeing to sponsor or champion something, ask why it's needed. Show your team you're curious about them and what they're doing. Very close to curiosity is the skill of listening. As the old saying goes, we have two ears and one mouth, so we should listen twice as much as we speak.

Humble

You may see a lot of egocentric leaders in the media, and you may question whether humility is really a quality that it takes to scale. I wondered this myself, and it's only within the past year that I had this epiphany. An egocentric manager will care about making themselves shine. A humble manager knows that we all have something to bring to the table and that by allowing others to shine, we're enabling them to bring their best.

Unless you've somehow figured out how to automate your entire operation, you know that you need a team to operate at scale. As you'll see in a later chapter, trust is an exponential power in getting teams to be productive. If someone is working for an egocentric leader, they know that at any moment, that person might turn on them or turn the spotlight on themselves. Only a humble person can be trusted.

Aha #10: A lack of humility leads to broken trust.

Lack of Humility → Inflated Ego → Self-Serving at the Cost of Others → Dishonest → Broken Trust

My friend Emily was really good at her job. She ran a small team of analysts, and her team was always the one picked for special projects because they always went above and beyond. Emily's boss let her do whatever it was that she needed to do. During their regular meetings, they would check in on priorities, and her boss would help remove obstacles. When Emily's team developed a new technology, her boss gave the team public praise.

Then, one day, Emily's company was bought, and her team was absorbed into a different division. Emily got a new boss, Johnny. At first, Johnny seemed nice, and he was really intelligent. However, Emily noticed that Johnny would often thank her privately for her work while he would take praise for himself in public. Eventually, she noticed that all the team's ideas were passed off as Johnny's. This was frustrating, but she understood that Johnny was leading the division. However, Johnny then started committing to unrealistic goals and leaving the cleanup for Emily and her team.

At first, Emily removed obstacles and helped out, but after a few months of doing all the work and receiving no reward, she got burnt out. Emily had a bright idea that she knew would take a lot of effort, but because her reserve tank was dry and she knew that she would be tasked with other challenges, she kept quiet and didn't share her idea. Her team started having more turnover because they were stretched too thin.

When the team didn't meet a deliverable, Johnny went to his boss and told them that Emily's team had failed. He didn't take account-ability for having put too much on them without getting them the resources they needed to complete the task.

Which manager got more from Emily and her team? Was it the manager who helped Emily shine and removed obstacles in her way, or was it the manager who took all the credit for himself?

As a leader, it's easy to stand on a pedestal, whether in public or private. It's hard to remember that a pedestal is made up of the sweat and tears of the team you lead and the stakeholders who helped set you straight. So, when you have an idea, it's hard to remember that it may have come through you but didn't come from you—and it's awkward to explain that to someone else.

The Leader Connection

Sure, if the idea is clearly someone else's idea, it's easy to give them credit. But so many other ideas come from so many people, and maybe you directed them down a path that enabled them to create a great idea. The lines get blurred.

In my travels, I often picked up leadership books and magazines. I remember reading a story of a guy who spoke about his team and how, when they succeeded, he would share the news as "We succeeded." When his team didn't succeed, he would share the news as "I failed." His example made me realize that I should never take credit for a team's success, even if I were the one with the idea. I also realized that if my team failed, then I failed because I was responsible for ensuring their success. I believe this paradigm shift has allowed me to scale over time. When a team succeeds, say, "We succeeded." When a team fails, no matter who was part of that failure, if you're the leader, say, "I failed."

There's a simple trick in leadership to replace the word "I" with the word "we" when talking about success. It works magic. As 17th-century English poet John Donne once said, "No man is an island." We're all products of the people around us.

Empathetic

If humility helps us see that there could be gaps, and curiosity helps us understand why the gaps exist, then empathy is how you fill in those gaps. Empathy is seeing a situation through another person's eyes. It's being compassionate and deeply understanding and sharing the feelings of others. Empathy is the gateway to having a different perspective. When we have multiple perspectives, we can see a better picture of the whole. This is what empathy allows us. Empathy allows us to get closer to reality. Truth is reality, but it's hard to see from any one perspective. My truth may not be the same as yours.

I find that when two people are in conflict with each other, if I listen to both sides with deep empathy, I can see how each person is true from their perspective. However, if I jump to conclusions without trying to understand the perspective first, I often miss the whole point.

Aha #11: When there's a conflict, the truth is usually somewhere in between.

Empathy and humility are both accelerators to scale because they open the door to trust, and trust brings speed to the workforce. Curiosity, humility, and empathy give us the perspective we need to see the big picture clearly.

Qualities That Lead to CONNECTION

The second set of qualities are those that lead to connection. In "See Good. Be Good. Do Good," this is the part about "being good."

Being is the connectivity of everything.

The scientific evidence for the connectivity of everything is plentiful. In chemistry, atoms connect to form molecules, and molecules connect to form compounds. Connected compounds form all known matter, which makes up everything in the observable universe.

In data science, we look at connections to determine causation and correlation. Two factors may be connected, but identifying whether they are linked in a causative fashion—meaning one causes the other—or a correlated fashion—meaning changes in one variable are associated with changes in another—helps us make better strategic decisions.

In physics, string theory is a theoretical framework suggesting that an imaginary string connects every particle. These particles are affected by the vibrations on the string, which are caused by interactions with other particles. String theory combines quantum physics with Einstein's theory of relativity, where time and space are interconnected. Despite its speculative nature, string theory has contributed to our understanding of cosmology and mathematical physics.

Let's look at religion. Connectivity is a central idea of Buddhism. In Judaism, Islam, and Christianity, G-d's chosen name for himself is hāyâ ăšer hāyâ, or I Am that I Am (Exodus 3:14). The Hebrew word selected for AM, hāyâ, is a continuous state of existence or of being.

Our job is to take what we've learned, process it through our lens, and pass it on. That's it!

Of course, it's that easy, and it really is, but it's also infinitely complex. Watch as I talk about the relationship of these two points.

A
B

Now, how many ways can these two points interconnect? The most obvious path is a straight line through both points.

A
B

The shortest distance between two points is a straight line. But that's not the only way to connect them. There are other ways to do this. Say, for instance, we add a third point, like so. Now there's a triangle of lines, and they are all connected. So, A and B are still directly connected, and they are indirectly connected through C.

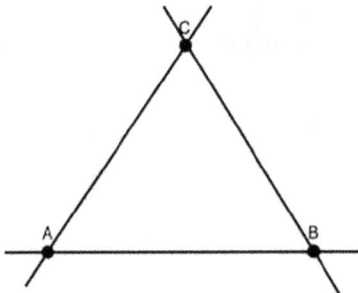

C

A
B

Now let's add another set of lines there; let's have a little fun. Look at all the additional connection spots where the first two points are connected simply because we added a third point to the picture.

The Leader Connection

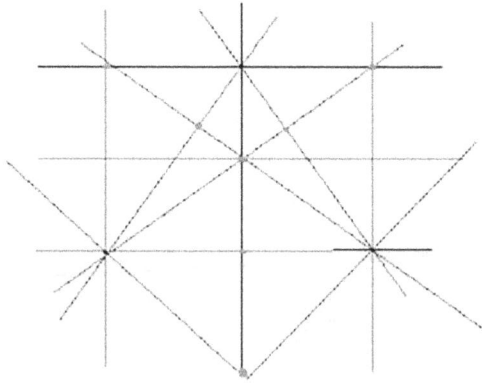

Let's make this 3D, which I cannot show you here, but imagine not only one more layer of this on top but an infinite number of layers. You can go out toward you, back behind the page of this book, right, left, up, down, or diagonal. Every point has an infinite number of planes that can pass through it, and they are all interconnected.

Now, let's step back to these two points. Knowing that all those lines exist in reality—we just cannot perceive them—we can now see that these two points are actually connected in an infinite number of ways. And that was using only straight lines! Don't even get me started on curves and waves.

A   B
●   ●

When you understand how everything is connected, you can scale much more easily and systematically because you know what levers impact the outcomes. The qualities I selected below not only support connection, but they are quick links to connections—the fast tracks, if you will.

Honest

Honesty is a fundamental connector, but even with honesty, there are different elements to consider. Honesty is like a compound element made up of four different atoms, the four Ts: truth, transparency, timing, and tact.

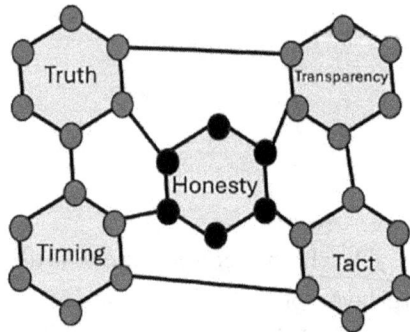

Truth: Truth is the simplest of all the elements. It's clear-cut. Because of other factors, you may not always clearly see the truth, but truth exists in the rawest of forms.

Transparency: Transparency is about how much truth we choose to show. Transparency requires education, explaining the WHY.

Timing: Everything has its time. There's a right time to know it, and there's a right time to share it.

Tact: You can be truthful without being harmful. This is called tact. Tact goes in a few directions.

Mark Twain once said, "If you tell the truth, you don't have to remember anything."

Truth is simple. It is what it is. But honesty can be hard in leadership because of the other three Ts. Let's dive into what makes honesty complicated.

Transparency often requires effort. We can't come out and say that we're not meeting our third-quarter targets without explaining first what the targets are and then what the drivers are that are causing us not to meet them. If we did that, we'd cause mass chaos. But we can say we're not meeting them if we spend the time discussing what those targets were and the challenges as they arose. When we do, we can course-correct and overcome the challenges. So, transparency is made more effective when you give people a WHY. Give people the WHY so that when you give them the WHAT, it's easier.

Time has two elements of complexity. First, knowing has a time. What I know to be true today may change when I receive new infor mation tomorrow. Take this situation as an example. Juan thought of himself as an honest leader. One day, his employee Anne told him that he wasn't always forthcoming. He was curious as to what she meant, so he asked her to tell him more about it. She then proceeded to tell him that he had told her he was going to stop the team from working on one set of releases and then move their focus to another priority. However, instead of stopping the releases, Juan had the team continue to work on them, which was creating a lot of effort that seemed unnecessary to Anne.

Juan was saddened at the realization that he had been on a journey that he hadn't taken Anne on. Previously, when Anne and Juan had met, she had given Juan two valid points, and Juan told her what he thought the next course of action would be, which was stopping the releases. Unfortunately, he hadn't thought about it again until he'd started pursuing what he needed to do to stop the releases. As part of that pursuit, Juan had met with a peer in another region. This peer had given him three new points that had changed his view entirely and made him realize that not only did he need to keep the releases, but he needed to release them faster. In his rush to get the releases out as quickly as possible, he'd forgotten to circle back to Anne to explain the new bit of information.

From Anne's perspective, he had told her one thing but done another. Even though he had been honest with her in the moment, it didn't feel that way to Anne.

As leaders of growing teams, it's important to keep the dots connected and the lines of communication open. Therefore, when you learn new information that changes your perspective, transparency requires you to share your knowledge with others so they can make the best decisions possible. This is why knowing has a time.

Sharing also has a time. For instance, if layoffs are about to occur, you can't tell people that they're about to be let go before it occurs. That could make an unsafe situation for the business or others around them. This is a legitimate concern and *why* confidentiality is critical until all the information is in place and messages are ready to be shared. In situations like this, rest assured that you can be honest with all players at the right time.

Tact, the final T, is difficult because it's more about the receiver than the words of the giver. People both give and receive appreciation and criticism in different ways. Being tactful doesn't mean being gentle at all times. You may have to be direct to be tactful because that's how that particular person best receives criticism. Being direct is not being unkind. Helping a person see what they need to see the moment they need to see it is kind. Be honest and direct in terms that the receiver can hear and understand.

Honesty is a connective quality because it leads to trust. If people see you being consistent with your approach, you will gain their trust. As you will see later on, trust is fundamental to your ability to scale.

Inspirational

People follow inspiration. Most people who have heard Dr. Martin Luther King Jr.'s inspirational "I Have a Dream" speech can attest to the passion ignited by his inspirational words. Jeff Bezos, founder of Amazon, is known as an innovative visionary. He's both a risk taker and has strong analytical skills, and he develops teams that are empowered to do the same. Inspirational leaders like Dr. King and Bezos instill hope in others. Hope leads to passion, and passion ignites people.

Aha #12: Hope in the workplace creates purpose and energy.

Hope is why we go on the journey. It's what helps us get through difficult times. A leader who instills hope will encourage their team to stick through the tough times. One way to create hope is to craft a vision that your team can get behind. When teams fall apart, it's often because the leader lost vision along the way.

Have you ever noticed that kids spend a lot of time and energy on things they're hopeful about? Just give them a giant cardboard box and notice how excited they get over the possibilities. You can create that same kind of childlike hope in your team by giving them a vision and something to aspire to.

Gracious

Aha #13: Gratitude is universal, but the format is personal.

I wrestled with whether to include graciousness as a quality or not because it is a byproduct of two others: humility and honesty. To be grateful, you humbly acknowledge that you fell short and accept with praise the gift someone else brings. In the workplace, we call it appreciation. Appreciation is not only acknowledging the past; it can also motivate your employees to future action, which is why this one is a force multiplier when at scale.

Have you read the book *The Five Love Languages* by Gary Chapman? Gary partnered with Paul White to write *The 5 Languages of Appreciation in the Workplace*. It's brilliant how they translated the word "love" into the word "appreciation" when applied in the workplace because that's how people receive their love, by receiving their appreciation.

As leaders, when we take the time to understand what each person is motivated by and use those motivations at the right time, we get a disproportionate return on our investments. If your employee is a "words of affirmation" person, a simple "thank you" can go a long way when it comes to sharing your gratitude. However, if the employee is not motivated by words of affirmation, "thank you" may not be enough. Imagine if Mira feels appreciated when she receives gifts, but her boss only uses words of affirmation. To Mira, words don't mean much, and all the "thank yous" her boss shares publicly and privately won't pay the bills or make her feel appreciated. When tough assignments arise, Mira, who already feels underappreciated, may not raise her hand to volunteer for extra work.

Merciful

Aha #14: Failure is a gift, and mercy is the bow.

The year was 1986, and I'd gotten a typewriter for Christmas. This wasn't just any typewriter. It had corrective tape in it, permitting me to make as many mistakes as I needed. I remember that summer well. Instead of going outside to play, I sat down at the kitchen table with the typewriter and began my first short story. It was the summer after third grade, and I wrote an adventurous mystery story with a magical tree in the backyard.

Looking back at it, the tree wasn't the magic sauce of the story; it was the corrective tape. Getting the opportunity to undo a poorly chosen word took the pressure off. Back when we used typewriters, there was an old trick to draw a line through the page before putting it in the typewriter so that the new page would be messed up, helping the writer overcome writer's block.

The same is true in work. When a leader expects perfection every time, people are less likely to rise to the occasion for fear of failure. But if a leader is supportive, even though there's a little bit of coloring outside of the lines, people are more likely to volunteer to color.

In other words, if you set your bar at perfection, people will be afraid that they won't be able to reach it. However, if you allow failure to be part of the learning journey and you allow your team to fail without criticizing them for that failure, they'll be more willing to go outside of their bounds and try something new.

Aha #15: Forgiveness encourages creativity.

Mistakes are a valuable learning tool. An environment that is forgiving when mistakes occur allows people the freedom to try new things and be creative. By now, everyone knows that failure is a path to success. You've heard the saying, "Fail fast." It's not intended to be the end of the story. You fail fast, so you learn from your mistakes and try again.

A connective leader understands this and creates a safe environment for people to fail. If you're not merciful, your team will be afraid of making a mistake, and they'll never try something new.

Qualities That Lead to APPLICATION

We've gotten through PERSPECTIVE, or *See* Good, and CONNECTION, or *Be* Good. Now, let's look at qualities that lead to APPLICATION. In other words, let's look at qualities that lead to action or *Do* Good.

Resilient

I imagine Moses from the Bible was one resilient dude. First off, the guy was raised with royalty, yet he gave up all that to help his people. When Pharaoh let Moses go, Moses kept coming back, bringing Pharaoh plague after plague from G-d, ten in all, until Pharaoh finally cracked.

You must have grit. As leaders, we sometimes get told, "No." When we do, we have to make a decision. Is this "no" forever? Was there a legitimate reason for it that we should have considered? Or, more likely, is this "no" for now? "No for now" is a very special kind of "no" because it eventually turns into a "yes."

Times change, circumstances change, and, watch me now, people change. Sometimes, the leaders who told you "no" move up, move out, or move on and get replaced with new people who will then tell you "yes." Often, the "no" we got was driven by a person's mental pictures of what can and cannot work.

So, when that person changes, strike again, and you may just find yourself with a "yes." This requires patience and resilience.

> In Moses's case, he didn't have to wait for the person to change. He had to change the person. In fact, what Moses did was a tactic I learned from Tony Robbins, a best-selling author and popular motivational speaker. Moses made the situation so painful that finding the "yes" was easier for Pharaoh than staying with the "no."
>
> Once Moses finally got out of Egypt, he traveled the desert for 40 years. For those of you who don't know this, his life is broken up into periods of 40s. He spent his first 40 years living in luxury. At age 40, he murdered an Egyptian for striking a Hebrew slave. This was a turning point in his story. From age 40 through 80, he was an advocate for the Hebrews, finally setting his people free when he was 80 years old.
>
> In the desert, people ate manna most of the time until near the end, when they finally got some quail. Did you know Moses lived to be 120? So, if you're following me, from 80 to 120, when most people find it hard to move around at all, Moses led his people through a desert, climbed mountains, built a majestic meeting tent, and created a judicial and leadership system for the Jews. That was one resilient dude.

Resilience is about being able to withstand difficult times. It's also about patience. When I was promoted to global center leader at IBM,

I wasn't prepared for the job. I was the best person available at the time. I had outlasted all my predecessors, who had decided to go exploring new territory.

Aha #16: Everything is skill, luck, and timing.

I had skills; I worked really hard to develop them. I had patience, which meant timing was in the bag for me. Patience leads to resilience. If you can wait out the storm, you will be better prepared the next time a storm rolls through. All I needed, then, was luck. And with time on my side, that, too, would be an eventuality.

Let's dive into some creative expressions using algebraic concepts.

Known:
Skill + Luck + Timing = Success
The subtraction property of equality:
*Skill + Luck - **Luck** + Timing = Success - **Luck***
Or Skill + Timing = Success - Luck
The obvious, but let's state it anyway:
Success - Luck = Intentional Success
Substitution property:
If Skill + Luck - Luck + Timing = Success - Luck
AND Success - Luck = Intentional Success
***Then** Skill + Timing = Intentional Success*

More obvious statements:
Constant Improvement + Time - Skill
         (constant improvement over time leads to skill)
Patience + Time + Resilience
         (patience over time leads to resilience)
The conclusion is drawn with some substitution and grace because these aren't numeric absolutes, but you get the picture.

A Well-Connected Leader's Qualities

Constant improvement + Resilience
→ Intentional Success

Voila. If you want a surefire way to intentional success, learn to build resilience.

Motivated

In the above equation, you need something more than resilience to get to intentional success. You need constant improvement. You have to be motivated. Being motivated means you are driven by a clear goal or purpose. Drive often shows up as passion. For this reason, this quality may show up in assessments as motivation, drive, or passion.

We talked earlier about gratitude being a motivator for others, and we looked at different ways to show gratitude. Management 101 tells us that different people are motivated by different things. That's helpful to know for your team, but this quality is about your own leadership style. When it comes to leadership, the person at the helm has to find their own source of motivation.

The question I hear a lot from overstretched managers is: how do you stay motivated when you're exhausted?

There are tons of motivational techniques. Here are just a few:

- Making goals
- Eliminating distractions
- Setting small goals
- Finding an accountability partner
- Developing a reward system that works for you
- Crafting a consequences system that works for you

Tony Robbins often talks about using pain for change. He explains that pain is a great tool for short-term motivation, while pleasure is a great tool for long-term motivation. To find out more on this, check out his book Awaken the Giant Within.

Aha #17: Change is a motivator.

While working on a project, I had to pull in a leader in my downline. I knew this leader was already very busy, but he was someone I knew could handle this particular problem. When I checked with him one day, I was surprised to find that he seemed to have a lot of energy for his new task. He was motivated. When I asked him why, he said, "Sometimes, change is as good as any vacation." This was something he had heard from a former manager. The more I thought about it, the more this idea resonated with me. Change gives people fresh eyes and energizes them.

For centuries, Buddhists have practiced the concept of shoshin, or "beginner's mind." This state of openness allows a person to experience life without preconceptions. It requires humbly accepting that you may not know what you think you know while also being open to learning new things. In his book, Zen Mind, Beginner's Mind, Shunryū Suzuki, a Sōtō Zen monk known for founding the first Zen Buddhist monastery outside of Asia, famously said, "In the beginner's mind, there are many possibilities; in the expert's, there are few."

When you change tasks, you get to start all over again. This refreshes you in the same way that practicing a beginner's mind does. It resets and rejuvenates you.

Sometimes, when your motivation doesn't align with the world's expectations, you have to create your own opportunities. In preparing for this book, one of the people I interviewed had led large-scale teams across South America. Throughout her career, she had grown in responsibility because she knew when not to take no for an answer. She cautioned that people need to understand the importance of taking risks. Sometimes, playing it safe is not going to get you where you need to be.

In the interview, she revealed that before she had been promoted into a regional leader, her boss told her that he would be moving to a new position. When she asked him what her role would be in the new structure, he said, "Nothing, really. You'll keep your job." He then told her that a new regional leader was opening, but she wasn't ready for it.

She replied, "Are you so sure that I'm not ready? I think I'm ready. What do I need to do to show that?" She spent the next several months proving why she was the right for the role. She got the job, but she told me, "This was me stepping up to a door that seemed to be closed. The door was there; I had to push it open." She had hoped for a bigger role, and that gave her the motivation to push open that door.

Creative

Mega-business leaders like Jeff Bezos, Bill Gates, and Steve Jobs are all known for their ingenuity and thinking creatively to find new solutions. Bezos challenged the logistics systems and turned it into a global machine that can handle two-day shipping, something neither the Post Office nor UPS could do at such large scales previously. Bill Gates, co-founder of Microsoft, created new ways of interacting with your computer, and he believed in software as intellectual property that could be licensed and commercialized. Jobs, co-founder of Apple, was interested in graphical interfaces, keyboards, and the computer mouse, and with the Mac, he redesigned the interface.

You might already know these very famous stories, so let me tell you something you may not know. Ingenuity is related to your ability to make judgment calls. The more complex the situation, the more we need our creativity to help our brains make connections. You can take the principles you've learned in one situation, apply them in another situation, and come up with something completely new.

AI has creative capabilities, but it still needs to be trained on lots and lots of data. The more complex the situation, the harder it is for AI to make the right "judgment" calls. Of course, AI is getting exponentially smarter the more we feed into it. However, your brain has something AI is not going to have in the foreseeable future. It has your experiences.

Resourceful

A close cousin to creativity is resourcefulness. Resourcefulness is not how creative you are with your ideas but how creative you are with using all of your available resources.

When I was in eighth grade, I had an amazing Spanish teacher named Mrs. Kowalski. As she went through her Spanish lessons, she'd weave in nuggets of gold here and there. She taught me something that I've used years later in my leadership, and I teach others.

Aha #18: Knowledge is of two kinds: that which you already know and knowing where to find what you don't know. – Mrs. Kowalski, eighth grade

I later learned that this was a paraphrase of an original quote by Samuel Johnson (from James Boswell's The Life of Samuel Johnson*), which states, "Knowledge is of two kinds. We know a subject ourselves, or we know where we can find information upon it." I'm not sure where it got simplified, but thank goodness it did. Simplicity supports clarity.*

Now that you know more about the qualities that lead to perspective, connection, and application, you might be thinking that you have several of them already. Good for you. I encourage you to think about which ones feel more natural and which feel less natural to you. Your natural qualities are the things that are deeply rooted in your value system, and you do them without thinking. Less natural qualities take a bit of work, but they're still masterable. Recognize your natural qualities for what they are—your gifts. How can you leverage these gifts? The qualities that are less natural to you are the ones you should develop.

Keep in mind what we're trying to accomplish together:

1. Perspective
2. Connectivity—or being
3. Application—or action, the "do"

Exercise 2: Identify your areas of strength and growth opportunities

1. For each of the sections above, *perception, connection,* and *application,* which quality is most natural to you? Don't neglect this; do more of it.
2. Now, which quality in each section is least natural to you?
3. Do you truly understand why this quality is important? To make this a stronger quality, you have to embrace the fact that it is a necessary quality. So, ask yourself, is this quality really important? Really try to understand why it's important. And if you didn't see it in my examples, are there other examples that you can find?
4. Can you identify at least three reasons why this quality would be a multiplier for scalability? Now, if you can do that, ask yourself how you can work on the quality that's the least natural. Give yourself a goal to work on and a timeline in which you will check in on your progress.

The Leader Connection

Summary: What you see leads to who you are. Who you are leads to what you do. *See. Be. Do.* How can we ensure it's good? By leveraging qualities that ensure we "see good, be good, do good." By being curious, humble, and empathetic, you set yourself up to have a wider lens, gaining more perspective. To strengthen your connectivity to others, be honest, inspirational, gracious, and merciful. But none of this matters if you don't take action, specifically the right action. That's where the qualities of application come in: resilience, creativity, motivation, and resourcefulness. As an added bonus, these qualities help strengthen and connect leaders to their teams, not only across small teams, but across large ones too.

Chapter 3
What a Well-Connected Leader Understands

"Do the best you can until you know better.
Then when you know better, do better."
– Maya Angelou

A well-connected leader understands:

- The Power of the Vision
- The Importance of Position and the Pointed Right Model
- Management Fundamentals

Remember this book reads like a study guide, with concepts building progressively in layers. You've just explored essential qualities that enable managers to evolve into leaders capable of growing teams and sustaining that growth. In this chapter, we will cover leadership and management essentials. If you understand these topics, you can skim this chapter for new content or skip ahead to more advanced concepts in Chapter 4. For newer managers, or ones that want some of those secrets to "working smarter and not harder," this chapter will help set you up for success ahead.

The Power of the Vision

Things are going to get hard, and there will be times when you get distracted. Your team will get distracted, too. Setting an effective vision statement will help keep the team on track. It's like a beacon that's always there when the storm comes. Even though things get hectic, if you steer toward the vision, you will end up where you want to be.

Let's make sure you have an effective vision statement before we jump into what else you and your team will need to be doing. Look at your organization. Treat it like you are the entrepreneur in charge. You've just been promoted to CEO, you've read up on the qualities that will make you successful in your new role, and you're actively reinforcing those natural qualities and expanding those qualities that are less natural to you.

As a CEO, you will be setting the vision or direction for your organization. Remember, your organization includes you and everyone who reports to you. Recognizing the importance of beginning with the end in mind, let's imagine what a thriving business looks like for you. You are now in charge of the vision and the strategy. You have also been given the keys to making your business thrive, the foundational principles of a scalable organization. Are you ready to build your strategic vision?

Exercise 3: How can your organization thrive? Create your vision and operational plans

1. What is your organization's unique value?
2. What need do you fill? This is your niche.
3. Who are your customers? Are they internal, external, or both?
4. How are you funded? Are you funded in internal dollars, cost of goods sold (COGS), or external dollars, revenue?

What are the dynamics at play in the external market, and how could that impact your funding?

5. How are you doing in sales today? How are you doing in sales tomorrow? You might be asking how you can determine that. Check out what your customers are saying about you. It's easy; ask them. If you're small enough, you can do this directly. If you need to, you can create a focus group or survey them.

6. What feedback have your customers given you that you haven't yet implemented? To better meet your clients' needs, is there something you need to change about your organization?

7. What's holding you back?

Can you create a strong vision around the answers to all the questions we just asked?

1. Now, once you've created that strong vision, who will you need on your team? Think of diversity, experience, and thought. Go back to Exercise #1 and see if there's anyone you want to include.

2. What do you need to do to empower your employees? How can you market your product or service to your clients?

3. What obstacles might arise? How would you handle these obstacles?

4. How will your team do what they need to do?

5. What tools and technology will you need for them to succeed?

These are your operational plans.

You now have the start of a vision. However, a good vision needs a vision statement that's easy to understand and repeatable. So, KISS Exercise #3 until you get a vision statement.

The well-known acronym KISS, or "Keep It Simple, Stupid," is so good that I considered making it an Aha. If you want someone to use it, it has to be user-friendly. I like to tell people that sometimes you have to grow through complexity before cleaning things up. Think of an iPhone; its popularity took off in part due to the ease of use of its interface. To make such a simple-to-use interface, a lot of thought must have gone into it, but they simplified, simplified, and simplified for the end user. I know there's a lot of rich content in this book, and I'm building layers underneath the surface, but I've also created a very simple user guide by following the Aha breadcrumbs so that if you wanted to peel away all the words in between and just read the Ahas, you'd still have something of value.

If you want someone to use your vision statement, it has to be user-friendly. If you're not 100% sure you nailed it, that's okay. As we stated in Chapter 1, a fundamental principle in life is that things change. Your vision has to have some room to change when you get new information that causes you to adjust your direction. Remember, you're going to begin with the end in mind, but you shouldn't be so rigid as to think you can't change your destination along the way.

The good news is that you don't have to know your end point from the start. If your destination changes, all it takes is a quick review of your current coordinates and a minor adjustment on your angle of trajectory, and you will still land in the new destination. The sooner you adjust your angle of trajectory, the less ground you need to cover in order to recover. This is getting pointed right. You get as close as you can at the moment, make progress, and then assess where you are and readjust your direction. If you do this, you won't ever get far off course.

The Pointed Right Model

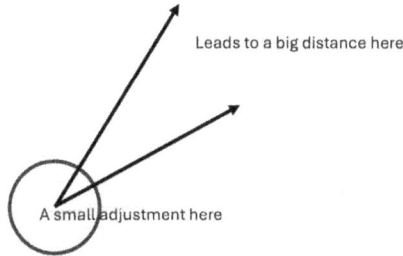

Leads to a big distance here

A small adjustment here

How far away is your end goal? The distance between you and your end goal is directly related to the size of the goal and the amount of change you will need to take your team through to get to that destination. In other words, the size of your vision impacts how much change you need to be thinking about. Whether you're more comfortable with small or big, it doesn't matter. Both will move you toward scale. However, as in financial investments, if you want to scale big, you need to risk big. If you want to scale small, you can risk small.

Business risks are just like investment risks, with upsides and downsides. You can reduce your risks in business in the same way you reduce your risks in investments. You can take calculated risks, which are still risks, but you have analyzed the data and removed as many unknowns as realistically possible. The market may be volatile on a daily basis, but when you zoom out, it averages an upside of 4% gains year over year.

People sometimes try to recreate this average by diversifying their market shares. You can do the same in business. If you have something that is earning you a certain number of "highly dependable" revenue dollars, you can identify how much of that revenue you can risk and still have enough to cover your operating costs and commitments to the street. But watch out! By diversifying your risks, I don't mean diversifying your income stream. At least, don't diversify income beyond what's sustainable. There's another principle at play in business: when there's too much diversification, it dilutes your ability to manage things at scale. As with all things, it's a balance.

If you want to go big, you need to have big goals—or even a big, hairy, audacious goal (BHAG). In their book *Built to Last: Successful Habits of Visionary Companies*, authors Jim Collins and Jerry Porras developed the idea of the BHAG, and big business leaders listened. A BHAG is a long-term target or goal that energizes an organization to focus its people, rallying them to a common cause and leading them through the process of transformation.

Connected leader moment: We've seen how sizing goals can relate to financial investments in that the higher the risk, the higher the reward. We also know the importance of risk mitigation. One of the ways investors mitigate risk is by analyzing historical trends over time and identifying accounts or stocks that follow similar patterns. Once they see a pattern emerge, they use predictive analytics to identify how the similar stock will fare.

> *We can do that in business, too. By analyzing competitors'*
> *growth and reduction practices, the local market trends, and*
> *historical market dynamics, we can predict which risks are less*
> *risky. Goals have risks in that they are not assured outcomes, but*
> *we reduce those risks by reducing the unknown variables and an-*
> *ticipating outcomes based on trends.*
>
> *When setting vision-statement-level goals, consider looking at*
> *goals set by companies in an industry that's similar to yours. Con-*
> *sider what successful companies' vision statements have been, as*
> *well as what unsuccessful ones have been.*

You now have a strong yet simple vision statement, and you have some goals for where you want your organization to go. However, before you set out on your journey, understanding a few key things about the journey ahead will help you pack the right tools and be prepared for when you get there.

Management Fundamentals

Whether it's your first team or your 21st, the foundation matters. I've led quite a few teams, and one thing I have realized the hard way is that when governance isn't built right at the ground and first-line leadership levels, the higher levels must constantly deal with escalation management. In this section, I have a few tips to help with ensuring success at that operational management level.

Aha #19: Always be willing, ready, and able to do the role that reports to you.

The only way to develop people to succeed in their job is to understand what it takes to do their job. Do you have to do it as well as your top performers do? Of course not, but you have to be able to direct them or coach them when you see something going off-course. There's a trick some leaders use when they don't know the role: they bring in an expert to help coach up their downline. That works well in the moment, but it's not sustainable long term, and here's why:

Let's say you have an expert making purple baskets, and they know what percentage of red and what percentage of blue is needed to get just the right level of purple. And now your whole team needs to make purple baskets, so you bring in this expert to show your team and don't learn the expertise. Eventually, your team starts making purple baskets, and they get pretty good. There's one person on your team who can put out more baskets than any other, so you tap them on the shoulder and ask them to show new team members how to make the basket.

What you didn't know is that this person is excellent at eyeballing the right percentage of blue and red, and over time, they stopped measuring it exactly. Because they were good, they just knew what to put in. They trained their new person but forgot to tell the newbie what to put in. Now you have lots of quality control points, but you cannot possibly measure everything, and one of the things you weren't measuring was the percentage of red and blue to get the exact color.

Of course you weren't. Remember, in this scenario, you don't even know the right percentage. You trusted your team to get it right. But people have moved on, and the knowledge you thought was being passed on was missed. Eventually, you'll get a whole different shade of purple.

Now, of course, you can avoid this scenario if the manager knows what the right shade of purple the baskets should be.

The trick is in a popular leadership cliché: inspect what you expect.

If, in your world, you have a million shades of purple, and it doesn't matter if they got the right shade, then there's no need to inspect that. You need to inspect what you expect—but you *only* need to inspect what you expect. A micromanager might inspect too much. A naive manager doesn't inspect enough. When a person has proven to you that they know how to do something and that they will do it when you are not looking, then you don't need to inspect what they are doing anymore.

> *Future-looking connection ahead:* When you get to the section on the Great Transformation in Chapter 6, you will learn more about the difference between growth-oriented teams and stabilizers. Once you do, I'll ask you to refine your lens when coming back to this Aha. While "understanding the role below you" works across both growth-oriented and stabilizing teams, it's more critical for stabilizers. For stabilizers, you need to know how things are done. For growth teams, you need to understand basic principles but not limit your team on how they achieve their results. The how is less important than the results for growth-oriented teams.

Aha #20: A manager should only do what ONLY the manager can do.

I heard this from a co-worker 20 years ago, and he heard it from a leadership training course. This one is tricky because you have to understand it right.

At first, when I heard him say this, I thought he was ignoring Aha #19 (always be willing to do the role that reports to you) and that he was crazy. I thought I was being helpful by rolling up my sleeves and supporting my team members whenever they needed me. Over time, I realized I was doing more harm than good. Not only was I wearing myself out, but I was also limiting my team's growth.

If you spend too much time doing other people's tasks, you don't let them develop. Like a helicopter parent, you enable bad behavior. In this stage, you risk getting stuck in firefighting mode because your employees don't know how to put out the fires themselves. There are two times this happens:

1. When others should do a task but can't, and you help them by doing it for them
2. When you have tasks that others can do but choose to do them yourself

For the first situation, even if managers do this from time to time, they understand why it's important to let an employee get their own experience. If this situation is one you're in, ask yourself, *Why can't the employee do this task? Is it resource constraints, education or something else?* When providing this kind of coverage, see what you can do to solve the source and put in guard rails to ensure the support you are giving is only temporary. Check yourself. If you're helping because you want to protect your employee from failure, then you're potentially doing more harm in the long run. Remember, the connected leader sees how failure leads to accelerated learning. By giving an employee the space to fail, we are giving them the space to succeed too.

The second situation is more elusive. Some leaders think that by doing the task, they are bringing value by carrying their own weight. They sometimes forget that their primary job is not to be an individual contributor but someone who develops others to their level. If you occasionally fall into this camp, remind yourself that your employees will never develop their own skills if you are constantly doing their tasks for them.

Aha #21: Shadows are the fastest way to cloning.

When you find that you're the only expert around and you're doing more than one job, your next job is to find a shadow. Take someone along for the journey. If you don't have time to build a training curriculum around what it is you do, let them see you in action. The trick here is to have them document what they have seen and share it back with you, and then you provide them feedback on their observations. This documentation can be the foundation for future training guides.

Now that we have your management structure in a good place, let's make sure your team is set up for the same level of success.

Aha #22: There's a science to roles and goals.

When it comes to building your team out, you want to leave very little room for error. In science, two basic quantifiers measure success: accuracy and precision.

Do you remember learning about accuracy and precision in science class with dart boards? The dart board with the darts near each other but off the bullseye is an example of precision. The one with the darts evenly spread around the bullseye, though possibly far away, shows accuracy. If you're aiming for the bullseye, you have to be both accurate and precise.

Precise but not accurate   Accurate but not precise

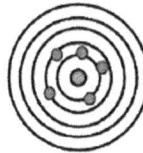

When you want to build out role models or job descriptions, you should aim for both accuracy and precision. If you very closely detail a job but miss the mark for what the job actually needs, you'll have a huge skillset gap on your team (precise but not accurate). If you are successful in hitting some of the elements of the job but not all of them, your team will be too dispersed (accurate but not precise).

Does this mean you need to define everything about a role before you get going? Not necessarily. But use the gray space wisely. Gray areas in roles and goals should not be by chance but by design. Gray areas can be used when you want people to have the freedom to venture out and explore new territory. This is where you're going to see your innovation and optimization occur.

The same can be true for goals. They should be both precise and accurate. I've found that the best way to think about goals is to align expectations with the role—everyone has to meet the role expectations. Expectations are an extension of the job description, but you should align goals with the right person at the right time. Goals change. Expectations don't.

Aha #23: What you measure is what you will get.

As a young department manager, I understood that our average flow-through rate was one qualified prospect for every 20 cold calls. So, I set a goal for my team members to each make a hundred cold calls a week. I assumed that would translate into five prospects a week, but it didn't pan out that way. Some people could generate 20 prospects in the hundred cold calls, while others only generated one or two prospects.

Then, in my research about how to report on hiring data, I ran across something from Albert Einstein, widely known for being one of the most influential scientists of the 20th century. He had famously written on his blackboard, "Not everything that counts can be counted, and not everything that can be counted counts."

I was counting calls, but what was also important was the quality of the source data and the interaction.

Management guru Peter Drucker says, "What gets measured gets managed." If the metrics chosen are not aligned with the organization's true goals, they can lead to misguided efforts. Also, there's a risk of overemphasis on quantitative data, leading to the neglect of qualitative aspects like customer satisfaction and innovation.

Because I was measuring volume and not quality, I got volume results that didn't translate into quality results. As Drucker predicted, what I measured was what my team was sure to meet. I was measuring the wrong thing!

Measuring the wrong thing creates more of the wrong thing. People will achieve what they are being measured against, but they won't focus on other aspects that are not being measured. What you measure will be the behaviors you create for the team. So, measure wisely to drive the behaviors you want.

The point is that as a department manager, you have to understand that if you want your employees to do something, you need to find a way to measure it. Also, you should not waste anyone's time by measuring what you don't care about. People will do the things they are held accountable for. If you're holding them accountable for the wrong things, they will focus their time and effort on those things because they are being measured against them.

Sometimes, we have the best intentions to measure things, but what we are measuring causes unintended consequences. Remember, you get what you measure.

Let me give you another insight that allows you to take this lesson to scale. I learned this from *The ONE Thing: The Surprisingly Simple Truth About Extraordinary Results* by Gary Keller and Jay Papasan.

Aha #24: Focus on one thing.

Find the one thing that when you do it, all the other things fall into place. In *The ONE Thing*, Keller and Papasan ask us to find our lead domino. Once we knock it down, everything else will fall into place. In management, this same logic applies. When we have too many focus points, we are spreading our effort across too many paths and either wearing ourselves out, or not achieving our goals. When setting goals for your team, what are the lead dominoes that will allow them to achieve all your expectations?

Let this sink in. You don't need 50 goals. You need one to three really good goals from which all the other goals fall into place.

What a Well-Connected Leader Understands

Summary: We learned about the Pointed Right Model. Beginning with the end in mind, we took a Management 101 course. Too many managers skipped this course yet were expected to ace the test. So, I developed a crash course where you learned about what you should and shouldn't do for your team. I shared a trick for creating clones when you're too deep in disaster recovery mode to stop the firefighting. We ended with goal setting and holding people accountable by measuring objectives and outcomes.

Chapter 4
The Fuel That Powers the Team

"If you want to find the secrets of the universe,
think in terms of energy, frequency, and vibration."
– Nikola Tesla

E nergy is what powers a team. Wouldn't it be great to know how to generate that energy when you need it most? To get energy, you need fuel. Where does the fuel come from? Well, that depends on which kind of energy you're trying to get. If you want kinetic energy, you need fuel that powers movement. If you want potential energy, you need fuel that increases your energy reserve.

*Science refresher alert: Energy is a scientific term. There are many types of energy, but they can be put into two categories or states of energy: **kinetic and potential energy.***
Kinetic energy is the energy that an object has because of its motion. It can be transferred from one body to another.

Potential energy is the energy an object has relative to other objects. It's a stored form of energy due to its position. It cannot be transferred from one body to another. Stick with me here and watch the connections.

Just as you can eat different foods to give you energy, there are different foods or fuels that you can use in business to give you and your team energy, too.

Kinetic Energy

Kinetic energy is all about motion. It's the DO in the "See. Be. Do" paradigm. Let's look at the qualities associated with the application: resiliency, motivation, creativity, and resourcefulness.

Perspective Quality	How You Can Support It	Why This Works
Resiliency	Encourage people to move outside their comfort zones and/ or take on stretch assignments.	Remember the journey story in Chapter 1 about the easy vs. hard path? You pick up new tools when you navigate new obstacles.
Motivation	Set a vision and goals. Identify individual motivators. Give people new projects to work on.	Motivation is the most direct energy source because it opens up the path from energy reserves to active energy systems. Think of motivation as a force acting upon a system.
Creativity	Encourage innovation with new solutions and designs. Don't get lazy with the status quo. Be careful not to shoot down ideas.	During creation activities, hope and excitement are generated. Creation activities can also develop new ways to innovate, which can reduce energy drain and create energy capacity.
Resourcefulness	Optimize	Optimization reduces energy drain.

The Leader Connection

This grid works for both individuals and entire teams. When you see people start to power down, one thing that really helps is to give them new projects they can look at with fresh eyes. Think about it. When you've been working on something too long and cannot find the motivation to keep going, don't you take a little break? Don't you pick up other things that are more interesting to you so that when you come back to working on your project, you have a little bit more energy built up? This is the kind of refreshing recovery that we will refer to in the upcoming section on rest.

Sometimes, the project is too big to completely set aside and work on something new. A helpful technique is to assign smaller projects that are not time-bound that your team members can weave in as they are working on the larger project.

Beware! If the inertia is too hard to overcome, people sometimes use smaller distractions that take them away from the larger project. You will see this when they seem to be prioritizing the wrong things or when the project isn't making progress at the pace you'd expect. When this happens, it might be helpful to break down the project into intermittent goals and sub-steps. You can use SMART (Specific Measurable Achievable Realistic/Relevant Timely) goals to set KPIs (Key Performance Indicators) that are indicative of whether the team member is on track.

In project management, we break up large projects into milestones that have target due dates, and we report back on progress toward those milestones. Do the same with your employees if needed. Schedule regular check-ins and hold your team members accountable. Accountability can help people stay focused. When they know that you're going to be checking in on their progress, they are more likely to prioritize effectively. You don't need to do this all the time. This tactic is best used when it's necessary to help someone stay motivated through a particularly daunting or complex project.

When people are metaphorically hungry, they are motivated. I was watching one of my daughter's soccer games, and the two teams were well-matched. Her team started out a little bit slow, and the other team scored the first goal. This completely deflated my daughter's team, and you could see it come out in their effort.

However, when they finally scored a goal, they got very motivated. In the last few minutes of the game, it was a nail-biter to see who would win. Both teams were hungry. Even though the girls were exhausted from over an hour of playtime, you couldn't see it on the field. In fact, the level of play had elevated to well beyond the level at the onset. They were motivated.

This is why engagement is so important in business. It's directly related to a positive financial outcome. When we can get people to tap into the bigger vision, when they genuinely buy-in, they become hungry to achieve the goals of the organization, which is directly related to income or profitability.

Potential Energy

To gain more potential energy in business, we need to build up our energy reserve or capacity for energy. One way to increase our energy reserve is by positioning and pointing right. Perspective gives us this advantage. How can we develop perspective with our team members, elevating their positions?

Perspective Quality	How You Can Support It	Why This Works
Curiosity	Continuously set up learning opportunities.	Learning is always an increased positioning tool. Learning additional skills that are aligned with the company vision helps team members get pointed in the right direction.
Humility	Provide group work.	The whole is greater than the sum of the parts. Leveraging each other's ideas elevates our own thoughts. This also increases positioning and perspective.
Empathy	Give people projects outside their core area of expertise.	Knowledge leads to compassion.

You give them better positioning, which increases their energy reserve. People get motivated by education and special projects. Educating them in the areas that interest them not only puts them in a good position to work smarter and not harder, but it also gives them hope for their future, and we just identified that as a form of fuel.

If our energy reserve is depleted, we need to replenish the reserve, and you can do that through rest and recovery.

Rest and Recovery

Energy comes in many forms, and guess what? Rest is a great way to gain energy. You can rest, but don't get lazy. Getting lazy is staying in "the zone" too long. Laziness is the opposite of forward progression because, through laziness, you can atrophy or even regress.

Rest is not lazy.

Aha #25: Rest, or active recovery, is a necessary action.

Think of there being two zones: an active zone and a rest zone. Staying in one of these zones for too long is what being lazy is, whether you rest too much or work too much.

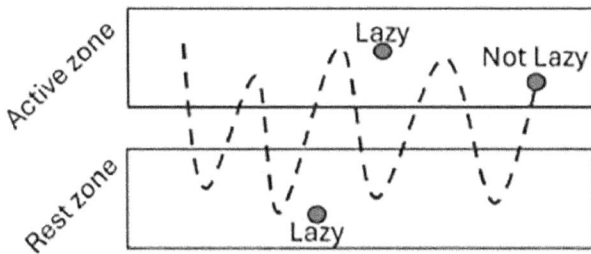

Yes, I just said working too much is lazy. Mind blown? Mine was, too, when I first discovered this. This is something I'm still struggling with, but I know it to be true because of the laws of nature and because I see it often at work. When you're busy, the easiest way to get yourself into a rut is to keep doing what you've always done, which means you end up saying yes to more before you've cleared out your backlog, and then you risk stretching yourself too thin.

In physics, the word "rest" describes an object not in motion. When I suggest you rest, I am really referring to recovery. Recovery is not motionless, is it? It's a recharging motion, and it's critical to your business success.

This recharging increases potential energy. When you aren't making room for recovery, you are not maximizing your potential energy.

Because this kind of recovery is active, you cannot stay in the "rest zone" for too long. Doing so will create atrophy and entropy. By being stagnant, you are going to lose what you've gained when you were actively moving.

Here are the science connections:

$p = mv$

Momentum = mass * velocity

Velocity = speed in a specific direction

Newton's first law of motion says that an object in motion stays in motion and an object at rest stays at rest. His second law of motion describes this as the force acting on an object is equal to its mass times acceleration, or

$F = ma.$

Momentum

Momentum is a growth accelerator for at least three reasons. First, momentum removes the need for force to overcome inertia. Second, when you "gain momentum," you are not moving at a constant speed but at an accelerating pace. This is what I call the momentum curve. Finally, when you are moving through challenges, you are growing and picking up new skills, which will enable you to be better equipped for future challenges.

The Leader Connection

Have you ever heard a leader say, "We can't take the foot off the pedal"? This phrase is so often used that it's almost overused, and user beware: there's a risk of burnout when you haven't allowed the team to venture into the rest zone. However, the intent of the phrase is scientifically solid. What it's referring to is that the team is moving in a direction, and the leader doesn't want to lose momentum. Momentum is that which keeps us going in the right direction.

If you want to move toward something faster, increase the fuel. For instance, you could increase the team's motivation, size, or computing power.

Here are the science connections:
$p = mv$
*Momentum = mass * velocity*
Velocity = speed in a specific direction
Newton's first law of motion says that an object in motion stays in motion and an object at rest stays at rest. His second law of motion describes this as the force acting on an object is equal to its mass times acceleration, or
$F = ma$.

During my research of various religious leaders, I realized that some of the most influential stayed in motion—moving between action and recovery, or meditation, and changing geographic location. Jesus constantly moved from one town to another. Muhammad went on pilgrimages. Buddha moved from the royal palace to the wilderness. They all went from areas of action to areas of relative quiet and inaction and then back. This wasn't inaction. This was an intentional movement toward growth. When they came back, they were stronger than before.

Aha #26: The momentum curve matters.

Some fuels, such as growing your team, increase speed at linear rates.

Here's why "growing your team" works with science:

In F = ma, m = mass. Therefore, if the object in motion is larger (the team), the force is larger. Increasing the size of your project also works, but it diversifies the team's effort and requires additional energy to sustain, so I didn't select it as an example. However, in certain situations, it could also be an energy-creation tool.

Other fuels increase speed at exponential rates. If you can get the momentum to move in an exponential curve versus a straight line, the team can feed the engine less fuel, relax some, and still gain speed.

Momentum in a straight line continues at the same pace, but momentum in a curve grows at an amplified pace.

The graph below shows the linear equation y = 2x and the parabolic equation y = 2x2. Notice how the curved line takes more time at the beginning to gain the same amount of innovation, but eventually, the two lines cross paths, and from that point on, the curved line progresses in innovation at a faster rate than the straight line. Your goal as a leader is to find the things that may take time upfront but will pay off exponentially in the long run.

The Leader Connection

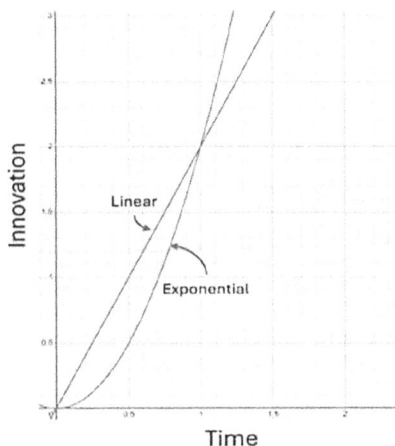

How can you get momentum going in a curved line versus a straight line?

Automation and optimization can help you achieve this. Chapter 7 will cover process optimization tools when we look at sustainable systems. Stretch projects and goals also achieve this because they grow your team at an amplified pace. Once they are stronger, they remain that way for future activities.

Another way to gain traction as you progress is to get into what Gay Hendricks, an American psychologist and author, calls "the genius zone." He introduced the idea of the "genius zone" in his book, *The Big Leap*. According to Hendricks, the genius zone is where your natural talents and passions intersect, allowing you to perform at optimal levels. I think of the genius zone as a freeway in the active zone. Not all activities in the active zone are motivating, but activities within the genius zone freeway are motivational. They give energy to the very project you're working on. Getting in the genius zone creates energy that fuels continued productivity. It's not an everlasting fuel, but it's certainly a boost.

Think about doing something you love. For instance, I can read leadership books for hours if I love the content. I could write for hours when I am passionate about it. In fact, in writing this book, I've found that I need to set aside blocks of time where I am not interrupted so I can unfetter the thinking flow of the genius zone.

Once a team is in the genius zone, a connected leader needs to be mindful of interruptions. Momentum has disruptors. There are many disruptors to forward movement in business, and it's the primary job of a leader at any level to remove obstacles.

If a second force interacts with the first force (F = ma), then you move in a different direction. Sometimes, in business, that additional force is unseen until it shows up. Sometimes, the force is helpful. Other times, it's an obstacle that gets the team off track. A manager's job is to identify as many of these obstacles as possible and remove them. The theme of removing obstacles reoccurs several times in this book, including in the chapter on execution as well as in the section on how to manage "break-fixes" at scale in Chapter 9.

Meetings have a special place in this chapter. They can be momentum disrupters, but they can also be momentum fuel when done right. The key to a good meeting is to always add value to as many of the participants as possible. Don't hold a group meeting if you're not adding value to at least 80% of the participants.

Meetings cross over between perspective, connection, and application. They allow you to strengthen the bonds of relationships and inform people of where they are and where they are going, and they remove obstacles along the way. However, all too often, we get into a meeting routine where there's a set meeting on the schedule, and we hold it regardless of whether it needs to be held. Too many of these, and you've reduced the value of meeting. Worse yet, you've broken the momentum curve of the employees who otherwise could be in the genius zone.

Exercise 4: Momentum/Don't Get Lazy

As an entrepreneur of your organization, your job is always to come up with a way to do what you do better, faster, and cheaper. Pick three functional areas where you will improve. If you are responsible for more than three functional areas, don't try to boil the ocean in a day. Pick your top three or one or two obvious ones. When you have made significant progress in these areas, you can always come back and add more functional areas later.

Use the grid below to identify how you can make each functional team work better, faster, and cheaper:

Functional Area	Improvement Opportunity	Opportunities to increase speed	Opportunities to cut costs

Now, with each of the above opportunities

1. Write down the very next step to making them happen.
2. Schedule the time to complete the very next step.
3. Schedule an appropriate follow-up time to check in on your progress.

According to standard mechanics, you can predict exactly what is going to happen to a particle based on its position and momentum. Remember, momentum also has a direction, or vector. It's the pointed right model! If you are in a specific position with a specific momentum, you will end up at a specific spot at a specific time. According to quantum mechanics, those particles, instead of having a position at a specific moment in time, are part of a wave.

Don't worry; I'm not going to dive into quantum physics, where particles might have multiple positions at the same time depending on how you observe them, but let's take a moment to connect this to business and leadership. When you know where you are now, where you are going, and what energy you need to get there, you can create any ROI you may need to develop the fuel systems to get you that energy. You've just followed the standard mechanics model.

Now let's add the quantum mechanics twist: you may not know all the other factors at play within your organization, which may prevent you from obtaining your objectives. That's okay; the particles move based on the observer. This tells you to account for your audience. Look into the specific initiatives that are important to your stakeholders.

Hopefully, you now know the importance of checking into broader corporate initiatives and understanding the interconnectivity of it all. When you can relate your initiative to the broader corporate initiative, you have a stronger chance of funding your request.

The Leader Connection

Summary: We took a short science detour in this chapter so that you could learn more about energy. After all, you need it to power your team. It was my intention that you understand there are different kinds of energy sources, and I shared a few tips and tricks on how to tap into them and how best to use them. Perhaps surprisingly, I shared how rest creates potential energy and is not lazy. I also discussed how the momentum curve can be an exponential accelerator because you are both leveraging the kinetic energy and gaining potential energy with momentum.

Chapter 5
What a Well-Connected Leader Does

"Well done is better than well said."
– Benjamin Franklin, *Poor Richard's Almanac*, 174.

A well-connected leader **executes well.**

That's it. Easy, right?

Unfortunately, it's not always so easy. If it were, two-thirds of all companies wouldn't fail before making it ten years. But you've got this. You're going to be in the third that succeeds because you're beginning with the end in mind and being thoughtful in your approach to leadership at scale.

Zig Ziglar, a prolific author and motivational speaker who wrote over 30 leadership books before his passing, says, "Aim at nothing, and you'll hit it every time." Agreed! The prior chapters were about making sure we got this right. We covered where we are and where we are going, and we added a few tools to our toolkit. Now it's time to release the metaphorical arrow and execute the plan.

Aha #27: Do nothing, and you'll get nowhere.

I once worked with a set of leaders. One was a planner; the other was a doer. The planner would see his target, and he would aim, aim, aim, aim, and he'd never shoot. The doer saw the target and shot, shot, shot all over the target, over and over again, and eventually hit the bullseye. Sure, there were errors all over the place and a few unfortunate accidents in the process, but occasionally, he landed quite well. There's a strategy that encompasses both: aim, fire, re-aim, and fire again. It's the same logic behind failing fast so that you can course-correct and then succeed.

When I was consulting with a healthcare company that was launching a new center, we knew we needed to create a go-to-market campaign to attract new talent to the organization, and we needed to do it fast, but we were stuck in the middle of an image transformation the organization was making. After a few weeks of discussion, we couldn't get anyone in the organization to sign off on marketing content that we had created because the organization had not finalized the new brand colors and fonts. They knew what their go-to-market message would be, but the colors and fonts were holding us up. We had run out of runway, and we needed to launch our recruitment marketing for a major job fair that would staff the new center of theirs. We made the marketing content in our own ads, and we took a chance, and it paid successfully. In the end, the executives were happy that we brought in the candidates that we needed to fill the roles. And no one batted an eye at the slightly off colors in the font of the marketing campaign that we used. No one approved it, but no one rejected it either.

This chapter has some Ahas that will help you remove the obstacles to "doing."

Aha #28: if it makes sense, don't wait for someone to give you permission. Do it.

You may have heard that it's better to seek forgiveness than to ask permission. Cultures with this kind of approach enable creativity and are action-oriented. They give teams informal permission to act. Sometimes, on the other hand, people get into analysis paralysis to where they don't do anything. And if it's your culture not to take calculated risks, then you'll end up in an environment that becomes outdated fast. Giving people permission to fail permits them to take a chance that may not play out the way you expect them to. It allows them to execute.

> *Connected leader moment: Mercy is a leadership quality that leads to connection. When you create an environment of execution, you have to be merciful when things don't go as planned. There's a story handed down by tradition at IBM of a salesman who made an extremely costly mistake to the tune of over one million dollars. The salesman was apologetic when he handed in his resignation letter to Thomas Watson, the CEO of IBM. Watson's response exemplifies the lesson of showing mercy and grace at scale. He handed the resignation letter back, saying, "Why would I accept this when I have just invested one million dollars in your education?"*

Larry Bossidy, the former chairman and CEO of Honeywell, understood this concept very well and created an entire culture around execution. In the book *Execution: The Discipline of Getting Things Done*, which he co-authored with Ram Charan, he explains that most strategies fail when they're not linked to business outcomes. This is the magic of beginning with the end in mind and aiming. You have to know where you're shooting for. That's the business outcome.

Your expected outcome becomes your business objective. It can be quantitative, but it also has a qualitative future. For instance, earning four million dollars is quantitative, but earning four million dollars while delighting customers is qualitative.

How do you measure how closely you are achieving your outcome? That's your key performance indicator, or KPI.

Exercise 5: Your business KPIs

1. Think about your organization. What value, service, or product does your organization create?
2. What would the result be from someone using you? How will they act or feel because they are receiving your solution?
3. What's your BHAG? Be specific with descriptors and timelines.
4. Break that down into 3-5 achievable goals, outputs, or phases that work towards your larger objective. These are your milestones. What is your very next actionable and realistic step for each? Put time limits on when you will achieve that milestone.
5. Now, summarize your business objective into one or two objectives.
6. How will you measure that?
   a. Think of at least one qualitative and quantitative measure for every goal. Be specific and measurable.
   b. Come up with two to five KPIs for each of your objectives. How often will you measure these?
   c. Put it on your calendar to come back and check in on your progress.

I knew the power of execution, yet I'm a planner and a thinker by nature. I analyze things. Thinkers are notoriously bad for their decision-making skills because they look for inputs that lead to clear conclusions. Generally, when a clear conclusion is not evident, thinkers will gather more and more input. When my pros and cons are balanced, you'll find that my pros have pros and cons sub-lists and that my cons do, too.

From Bossidy and Charan's book, I knew that if I didn't strengthen my decision-making skills, I was never going to create a culture of execution. The first step to execution is knowing what the objective is; once you've done that, you can act on the objective.

Connected leader trick: Remember the pointed right model? Your decision determines your direction, but your direction doesn't have to be final. For thinkers, this is very freeing because it means your decision doesn't have to be final. You can make the best decision now with the most available bits of information you have, and then, when you have new information, you can adjust your decision and refine your direction. Small improvements along the way turn into large improvements later on.

The very first step is to point and go. If you wait for all the right inputs, one of two things will happen: 1) you won't ever leave the starting line, or 2) someone else will beat you to the finish line. This is the problem with the analysis-paralysis mentality that so many thinkers find themselves in. However, by making a decision that you know you can change, you remove that obstacle to execution.

In his 2016 letter to the shareholders, Jeff Bezos says that you should make decisions when you have approximately 70% of the inputs needed, knowing that down the line, your decisions could change.

Here are the steps to take when combining the Pointing Right Model with the Execution Model:

1. Identify what the objective is (make a decision).
2. Identify what it would take to get to that objective (these are milestones).

3. Set SMART goals for the milestones (these are your KPIs).
4. Identify what's the very next best thing to move towards your first milestone.
5. Do it.
6. For each milestone, rinse and repeat until you've achieved your objective.
7. If, along the way, you are not meeting your KPIs, identify what you need to adjust OR take the new input to adjust your objective so that it is an achievable and realistic goal.

It's okay to reassess and start over again. Removing the fear of making a mistake is extremely empowering.

So, you've made a decision. Now what?

I remember reading David Allen's *Getting Things Done*, and if I'm being honest, I was struggling with the book. I knew it was going to be powerful if I just stuck with it. Through the book, he told me that it would take some time to get myself organized, but once I did, it was going to pay off.

So, I took a couple of days off of work to really devote the attention he had requested of me and follow his advice. I went into my home office, which is not only where I keep business things but also where I keep my personal records, such as finances, medical records, and things for my family. I put everything in the middle of the room, and I turned my world upside down.

Here's what I do today. It's not fully following Allen's method, but it's effective for me.

All my pending actions go into a tracker. My main trackers include

1. Email
2. A to-do list

To-do list: I have done a master list, and I have kept separate lists based on the topic. Which do I prefer? Well, that depends on how many items are on my list. When my list is not long, one master works best. When my list is very long, keeping separate lists grouped by topic works best for me.

Now, to execute my actions, here is the flow I use:

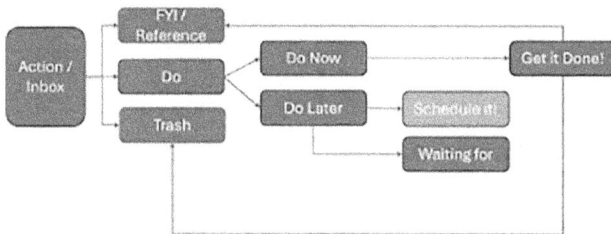

The secret sauce is the scheduling trick. If you don't do it immediately, you need to take a moment to schedule it so it will naturally come up again. This is the file-and-forget-about-it method. It allows you to clear space in your head to think about other things so you're not carrying the weight of the unactioned item with you.

When I'm in my groove, I keep my mailbox at the elusive "inbox zero" with this method. I get hundreds of emails every day, as I know many of you do. Before applying Allen's method to my inbox, I couldn't keep up with it. Plus, I would attend anywhere from seven to ten meetings every day and would find myself in back-to-back meetings where I had to go from one to another, making commitments. At the end of the day, I had all these actions piled up that I couldn't get done during the day because I was in meetings. So, I'd begin the second half of my day at 5 p.m. when most of the meetings were over. Sound familiar?

I would find that my average day was anywhere between ten to 16 hours a day. This went on for months and months. If I'm being honest, it probably went on for years. Of course, I thought I was working smart.

Originally, I organized my email into themes. These themes would change according to the projects I was working on and the clients I was consulting with. At any one point in time, I'd have ten to 20 folders to organize my emails into. If the email were an FYI or something I needed to reference later, I'd file it away. If it needed an action, it would sit in my to-do box until I actioned it.

You all know how this story ends: in a mess. I have no doubt I was not alone. My inbox had thousands of emails that never got cleaned up.

Then I changed my filing method to two folders:

Folder Name	What Goes In It
To Do	Anything that requires action—whether it's scheduled or I'm waiting on something before I can action it.
Read	These are all my FYI items that I want to keep for reference. My completed actions go here.

Sometimes, within my to-do folder, I put a "follow up" folder—these are the things that I was waiting to hear back on from someone else, and the idea was that if I hadn't heard from them in a timely manner, I would follow up. But the reality is that this didn't work so well for me, and that "follow up" folder would grow because I never did my Aha #29.

Aha #29: Do it. If you cannot do it now, schedule it.

If you can do it now, do it, but if now is not the time, schedule the time to do it. Sometimes, there's not enough time to do it now. Other times, I need to think about the steps that are required to get it done. Both those times are great opportunities to block time to take action.

Instead of my "follow up" folder, I now move those items into my "read" folder (I use my read items as a reference folder, but you can trash these if you'd like), but I mentally separate which of those items need my nudge and which do not. I find that anywhere from half to three-fourths of the items have next actions with someone who is both capable of doing the job and mature enough to close it off with me. Those items, I can trust someone else to handle, and therefore, I can get them off my radar.

For the remaining quarter to half, there's an unknown element that requires my follow-up, and I schedule those to check back in. The flow looks like this:

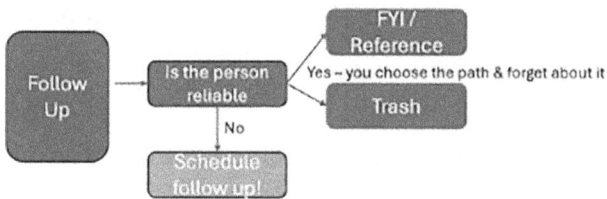

Here's why I'm able to delete half my follow-up using this method. Remember Aha #20: A manager should only do what only a manager can do. If the employee is able, then the job is theirs. I don't need to follow up to ensure they have done it. We will see this show up again when we visit the Situational Leadership model in Chapter 7.

The trick to keeping the to-do folder from piling up in my inbox is that I pair emails with a calendar block of time to action the email. If I have several emails that I need to plan the course of action for and I don't know the first step for the block of time, then I bucket all of those into appropriate chunks of time to process an action.

Since I'm no longer worried about what I still have to do because it's already on my calendar, I can drop the burden of the worry from my mind. The unexpected impact of getting my emails and next business actions calendared was that it got rid of the worry that was weighing me down. Without the burden of keeping so much in my head, I became even more productive. It also gave me more energy because carrying the load of my to-do list was draining my energy.

Congratulations! You've just raised your potential energy levels.

Once I blocked off that time in my calendar, people didn't schedule meetings during that time, and my workday got shorter. You will need this technique if you want to scale without burning yourself out. It's the soft no. An open calendar is a "yes" to whatever anyone wants to put on. A closed calendar is a "no" to new learnings. The trick is somewhere in the middle, forcing people to prioritize your time over theirs.

Aha #30: Your time is an important resource. Take ownership of it.

People will always schedule meetings based on their needs over yours. It doesn't matter if the meeting is urgent or important to you; they will schedule it based on how they prioritize the meeting within their availability. If they have an action they need to get done first, they'll push the meeting out. If it's urgent to them, they'll prioritize their time for it. This is because they know what their priorities are and don't know what your priorities are in relation to your available time. They only have your availability.

I found that if I blocked my action time, people didn't mind waiting. If I had available time and they were available at the same time, they'd take that block. But if I only had 30 minutes available in a day to do my own action items and they were free at that time, they would take that 30-minute block even if the call could wait a couple of days when I had more time free to do both. But when my time was blocked by my planned actions, they were usually happy to wait until I was available. If they had something really urgent, they would reach out to me directly, asking for flexibility. I regained control of my time.

Someone once told me that my inbox was made up of someone

else's to-do list. The more I thought about it, the more I realized that they were right.

The emails that I get are sent to me because

1. Someone wants me to action something.
2. Someone wants me to know something.

While well-intended, our fear of missing out causes us to prioritize all wrong.

I knew my priority list, but I was letting other people's priorities distract me from getting my work done.

Have you ever seen the Eisenhower Matrix, where, on one axis, you have "URGENT" and, on the other axis, you have "IMPORTANT"?

	Urgent	Not Urgent
Important	✓ Do	📅 Schedule
Not Important	👥 Delegate	🗑 Delete

When you bucket your emails into actions that you schedule later instead of actions that you're taking right away, you're freeing up your immediate time for the urgent and important activities that you also have scheduled.

What are you prioritizing? In my line of business, we get new projects, new accounts, and new requests for analysis all the time. There's always something new coming in before the old stuff is fully done. When I say yes to everything, I end up not having enough time for anything. So, I need to select my priorities and say yes to those. But no doesn't mean that the work doesn't have to get done. It just means I don't have to be the one to do it. Is there someone else who might enjoy this work? This would be a good opportunity for them.

Aha #31: Instead of "No," find the "Yes, AND."

To take control, you have to be able to say no. But in business, people don't handle getting no for an answer very well, especially if those people are your leaders or clients. So, there's another kind of soft no that's my favorite, and it's the power of "Yes, AND." Instead of saying no, find a way to say yes, which usually requires that you pair it with an AND for you to find a win-win. You'll need something from them that will enable your success.

Can you deliver the work? → Yes, AND you need to provide me with the resources to do so.

Can you meet this really insane timeline? → Yes, AND we won't be able to give you all the bells and whistles, so which bell and which whistle do you want me to remove? OR Yes, AND in order to do so, I need to down-prioritize something else; which should that be?

Can you research this content for a sales pitch? → Yes, AND Johnny will do the legwork before I review it.

Sometimes, there's a layer of ANDs
Can you hire five hundred people next week? Yes, AND it will cost a lot of money, AND you are going to need to lower your requirements.
And sometimes, you can throw an OR in to give them options

Can you build a supercollider? Yes, AND it's going to take a long time. I'll need you to help me make space in my calendar to learn how to do it first. OR I could connect you with this third-party provider who has done it a number of times, and you can have it even faster.

Just because someone is asking you to do it, it doesn't mean you are the one who has to do the "do." You're the one being tasked with making sure the "do" is getting done. If you're the department manager or have aspirations of becoming one, you need to know this. Being the hero is likely what got you to the job, but if you keep trying to be the hero at this level, it's going to be your downfall.

Your job now is not to be the hero but to develop a team of heroes. Being a hero is the blocker to scale. Heroes are amazing characters that we all love, but they need problems to be heroes. They're also the single point of success. Being a hero at work means people will always come to you. So, if you find yourself not wanting to say yes, ask yourself if there's a "Yes, AND that's a great opportunity for Piotr."

What happens when you need to find the yes but don't have the skills on your team to do it right now? That's when you need to fill in your gaps.

Aha #32: Build, buy, or outsource.

Companies grow through two main paths: they either build what they need or they buy it.

To build it is called **organic growth**. This is where a company expands by increasing its internal capabilities. When a software company develops new software, that's an example of organic growth.

To buy is called **acquisition growth**. Companies often buy another company that can bring a component they need. For example, IBM often buys other companies to leverage the expertise others have already built instead of spending the money to develop that expertise in-house. This allows them to quickly move past the trial-and-error stage that occurs when growing from within and leverage their capital to acquire a company that's gone through it before.

Another way companies grow is through outsourcing or using **strategic partnerships.** If they don't have the resources to build from within—and sometimes, that resource is not money but time—and they don't need to buy what they need because it is not part of their core offerings, then, sometimes, it's best for them to find a strategic partner who can bring them the growth they need.

Aha #33: Growth strategy is based on any combination of the build, buy, or outsource model.

Even though this may be obvious, it's not easy.

What they do is an important consideration of connected leaders.

They see the connection between the return on investment on whether they buy, build, or outsource.

Building, of course, refers to building the infrastructure within a company.

Buying in the business world would be acquiring a company that already has the infrastructure in place. This is a great move if you need an offering now and don't have the time or resources to build it.

Outsourcing is finding a partner who provides the offering for you. This is a great option when the offering is not in your area of expertise or primary revenue stream. A lot of business outsourcing is done by groups that fall in the COGS (cost of goods sold) category, meaning they need to deliver something, but there's a cost to deliver it. When you outsource it, you often spend less and get better quality than you would by doing it yourself because you are paying for the expertise.

If your gap is in your go-to-market offering, you need to build it or buy it. Outsourcing is not an option.

Build, buy, or outsource can be more than just about building out company infrastructure. If you take the management-level view and look at where it can be applied elsewhere, you'll see it can be used in all your gaps.

As an individual contributor:

Don't have the right skillset? Build, buy, or outsource.

As a manager:

Don't have the right team? Build, buy, or outsource.

As a director or above:

Don't have the right product line? Build, buy, or outsource.

This even works at home:

Don't have dinner? Build, buy, or outsource.

Don't have a car? Build, buy, or outsource.

Don't have time for transportation for your kids to get to and from their events? Build, buy, or outsource.

Summary: Chapter 5 is dedicated to the "do" part of the See. Be. Do. paradigm. Execution is the difference between dreaming about your goals and achieving them. We looked at what obstacles sometimes get in the way of execution and how to eliminate them. I gave you some email insights and also the gift of understanding the power of "Yes AND." We also talked about various ways you could execute, whether that be through your own team by building or buying the necessary resources, leveraging other specialized teams, or outsourcing.

You have now completed the foundational work for setting up your team to scale successfully. Are you ready to take that leap to the next level? Let's get started by learning about the Great Transformation.

Chapter 6
The Great Transformation

"When you are finished changing, you are finished."
– Benjamin Franklin

Have you ever noticed how, in some company cultures, people tend to cc almost everyone in emails? Because I work with so many different companies, I wondered why, in some places, I could work directly with one person, but in others, when they replied to my direct email, they copied five more people. I thought this was a sign that the company had a culture of escalations and that I needed to tread carefully, but now I realize it's often due to specialized environments.

What I mean by that is that the company has a group of specialists who understand their remit quite well, and the people in the emails were all specialists who were looking at the email with their lens. In contrast, in smaller companies, people tend to handle a wide range of tasks themselves, leading to fewer boundaries and less need for extensive communication.

The Great Transformation

In such small settings, people are used to working with agility and wearing many hats. People manage a range of functions on their own, so they only need to communicate with a few others. They are able to make decisions in isolation. These are the companies where it's somewhat easy to bring ideas to life.

However, the employees within companies like this are often very stretched and constantly climbing uphill. The entrepreneurial spirit has been associated with a no-bull, get-stuff-done mentality. It's also associated with working long hours and a lot of tough but engaging work.

This led me to wonder: what is it about scale that causes such vast differences in ways of working?

To grow is simple. There are two rules to growing your business.

Rule #1: Do what sells.
Rule #2: Don't do what doesn't sell.

I said it was simple, not easy. There's a responsibility around doing what sells. Just because something sells, it doesn't mean it's ethical or beneficial in the long run. Still, growth requires market demand. Sustaining that growth is difficult and requires an operational transformation. As companies grow, teams become more specialized, and reliance on others increases. Boundaries become crucial, but they are rarely as black and white as they seem. Effective communication becomes essential. It's in these specialized environments where ideas more easily die. A person has an idea and shares it with many people. Each person adds their own spin, and the idea grows into something difficult to achieve. Eventually, it gets rejected by one of the many teams that must approve it—teams with competing priorities, such as logistics, finance, or compliance. As a result, the idea never takes flight.

Now, that's not completely fair to large organizations; they are able to pull off very exciting ideas, but I'd venture to guess that more ideas die that could have been brought to life in more agile environments. To be fair, diversifying the company's direction is a danger to the broader objective of large organizations. The other thing that happens in large organizations is that the ideas that do take hold often take longer to bring to life due to the necessary governance that has been indoctrinated into the company.

Here's the difference between small companies and large ones. Small companies are nimble and agile. Because few people wear many hats, they have a broad understanding of the inner workings of the business. Individuals can make big decisions across a vast array of topics. In large companies, on the other hand, breadth necessitates specialization. When you have large amounts of specialization, you have to slow down for vetting and communication. You will also have different perspectives to contend with, which makes decision-making more tedious and increases the risk of innovation getting lost in approval chains.

Small and Nimble → Large and Specialized

To maintain the agility of small companies, some large organizations create smaller, entrepreneur-like units within them. While this approach fosters nimbleness, it can also lead to silos. These mini-companies often struggle to communicate and collaborate effectively with each other. Most companies want to stay small and nimble, and not many make it to the large and specialized arena.

According to a series of studies published by the Bureau of Labor Statistics, only 44% of companies last four years. According to an extension study put on by NYU, only 31% of companies last seven years. With such low survival rates, wouldn't it be nice to know what's happening here and what the trick to survival is?

The lead researcher of these studies, Amy Knaup, says there's a correlation between survival and growth of employment rates, meaning the companies that grow and scale are the ones that survive. These companies adapt to changing demands.

But what if we don't want to just survive? What if we want to thrive? Isn't that what's needed to scale a business?

The Great Transformation

The U.S. Chamber of Commerce has identified characteristics that cause a company to thrive. Chief among them are:

- Willingness to take chances
- Unique value
- Tenacity
- Customer-centric approach
- Good marketing
- Strong vision
- Passionate leaders
- Empowered employees
- Adaptability
- Diversity

Let's draw some connections between the characteristics of thriving companies and the connected leader qualities I highlighted in Chapter 2.

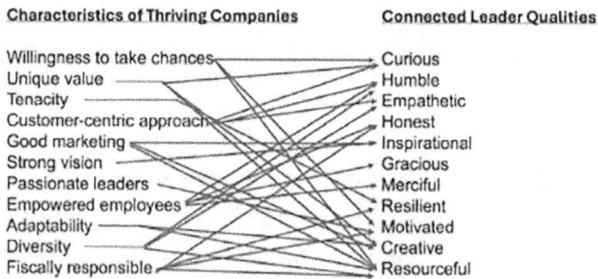

Characteristics of Thriving Companies	Connected Leader Qualities
Willingness to take chances	Curious
Unique value	Humble
Tenacity	Empathetic
Customer-centric approach	Honest
Good marketing	Inspirational
Strong vision	Gracious
Passionate leaders	Merciful
Empowered employees	Resilient
Adaptability	Motivated
Diversity	Creative
Fiscally responsible	Resourceful

What can you do with this information? Knowing that these are characteristics of thriving companies, we can securely assume that they should be foundational principles of a scalable organization. These characteristics of a thriving business are the principles on which you should build your business model.

Connected leader moment: Think back to what we said in Aha #7: Your foundation sets you up for your future. You just learned about a foundational principle for a scalable business. The attributes above set apart successful companies from those that fail. Bookmark this.

Did you notice that I added "fiscal responsibility" to this list? There's a reason for that, and it's all about our C-suite.

The traditional C-suite has

- Chief Executive Officer (CEO): In charge of the vision and strategy
- Chief Human Resource Officer (CHRO): In charge of the people and communicating culture
- Chief Financial Officer (CFO): In charge of financials
- Chief Operating Officer (COO): In charge of operating procedures
- Chief Technology Officer (CTO): Oversees the use of technology
- Chief Marketing Officer (CMO): Oversees go-to-market strategies. This includes marketing and advertising, but in many companies, it also includes sales strategy

You need to understand what each of these people is responsible for because whether you have a team of ten or a team of a hundred, you will need to have a good handle on each of these elements.

Connected leader moment: Look back at the questions I used to help you set your vision and operational plans in Exercise 3. Can you see connections in how those questions mirrored the roles of your C-suite? This was no accident. History gives us the answers, and the answers give us the questions we need to ask ourselves.

As a CEO, you must share the vision and direction of your company. In your strategy, you will care for the people, culture, finances, operating procedures, technology, sales, and marketing. How do I know this? It's something companies have prioritized by having a senior leader oversee it—it's the C-suite.

All companies that scale will go through a transformation that I call the Great Transformation. This is not a one-time event. It's an ongoing activity.

I imagine the Great Transformation to be like what happens inside a star. At the star's core, nuclear fusion occurs, where hydrogen atoms bond to form helium. In an organization, I equate nuclear fusion to the service or product, whatever the company is selling. It is the force causing the company to expand. But, as with a star, if the company were to expand without stabilizing, it would either come apart or collapse. The star maintains its balance by hydrostatic equilibrium, where the outward push of energy created by nuclear fusion is overcome or balanced by the inward pull of gravity, allowing the star to be stable. Companies, like stars, have to also pull together and reconfigure on the inside while they are expanding on the outside. They have to maintain equilibrium, not only despite the expansion, but also because of the expansion.

To understand what's happening in the Great Transformation, let's take a brief look at history and explore two leaders who created vast empires in short periods and made significant impacts on history, several of which we still see today: Alexander the Great and Genghis Khan.

Alexander the Great, born in Macedonia circa 356 BCE, was one of history's most illustrious military leaders and conquerors. He was well-educated, having been tutored by Aristotle. Over approximately 15 years, he established one of the largest empires, stretching from Egypt to India, encompassing Greece and the Middle East.

Growing an empire rapidly was no easy feat. Beyond his conquests, Alexander had to ensure the stability of his expanding territories to prevent mutiny. To maintain control, he promoted the blending of Greek and local cultures, a process known as Hellenization. He also promoted marriages between his military and local women and adopted local customs, all the while spreading Greek teachings. He was unwavering in his requirement of governance to maintain the area he had conquered, but when it came to governance, he took a flexible approach to reduce chances for retaliation. He retained local rules and customs and integrated them into his administration.

Genghis Khan was not only the founder of the Mongol Empire (circa 1206), which was the largest contiguous empire in history, but he also connected the West and the East by supporting trade between China and Europe along the Silk Road. Genghis Khan was a shrewd military leader who led a group of nomads as they conquered a vast array of lands from the Pacific Ocean to Eastern Europe.

However, once Genghis Khan left a conquered territory, he had to figure out how to maintain the lands he had conquered. So, he set up a series of laws called the Yassa, which were standardized across the empire. He practiced religious tolerance and allowed people to maintain their religious beliefs, removing the need for unrest and rebellion. He also included conquered people in his army and allowed them to be promoted along with anyone else who had earned the right. This was a significant change, as, previously, promotions had been based on birthright rather than merit.

In a book about scaling teams, I couldn't leave out these kings of scale. Let's tease out some similarities between these two leaders:

1. Strong vision
2. Very passionate
3. Explored and conquered new territory
4. Empowered their military
5. Enforced a unified governance over conquered territory
6. Fiscally responsible
7. Adaptable
8. Inclusive (Ok, I am not imagining Genghis Khan and Alexander the Great as big ole teddy bears, but at least they let people practice their own customs and integrated their military with the locals.)

Connection moment: these leaders share many characteristics with the thriving companies we just discussed. Observing the approaches of these two leaders, we see how nomads gain their territory and interact with the settlers who were already there. This dynamic represents **the Great Transformation: an ongoing shift between growth-oriented and stabilizing teams.** In businesses that survive beyond 10 years, a culture of balance between these two forces is essential.

Consider it like the star that must both expand (nuclear fusion) and contract (gravity) to maintain stability. This analogy underscores the idea that change is constant. To navigate this change, leaders need to be agile. Let's delve deeper into these two interdependent dynamics to uncover insights that can help us, as leaders, support both constructs.

Nomads and Settlers

Nomads

Innovative teams are like modern-day nomads, constantly seeking new territories to conquer. These agile groups, often composed of individuals wearing multiple hats, excel at thinking creatively and discovering new opportunities. They thrive on claiming new revenue streams but seldom pause to establish sustainable systems.

Today's nomads are out-of-the-box thinkers who flourish with minimal rules and ample space for creativity. They are hunters, always on the move, and prefer not to settle down. They may not handle the rigor of rules and constraints very well. They flourish with fewer rules and guidelines and lots of room to be creative.

But a leader's challenge is that once you get outside that box, you need to build a new box around the new territory to sustain it, and nomads aren't likely to be the ones to create this new set of guidelines for long-term sustainability. Nomads don't like staying there. They like being nomads. So, you need someone else who can settle down in the new territory.

Settlers

Once a new territory is discovered, settlers—your established team—can take over. They like the security and familiarity of the box, the same box that the nomads needed to explore outside of. Just as settlers need sustainable sources of food, clothing, and shelter, established teams must find resources that will sustain them.

Settlers thrive in organization and process. They need security and a clear vision for the road ahead. As they settle in, they become tradesmen. They organize themselves into specialized roles and figure out how they can leverage each other's expertise to maintain stability in the community.

Because they spend time developing deep expertise, they can take something small and grow it into something large when they work together. They will cultivate what is around them and make it much greater than it was before they got there. This is something nomads are not able to do because they do not develop the deep expertise that the settlers do.

In business, there are two types of teams and ways of thinking about growth and sustainability.

In growth-focused teams, often found in new teams and innovative teams, you've got nomads who like exploring new things, i.e., generating new revenue. In sustainability-focused teams, often found in established teams and operational teams, you've got settlers who thrive in stabilized systems and governance.

To scale, you need **both**. This is what Alexander the Great and Genghis Khan taught us. You need to support both mentalities and find some way to get the two working together. You need to be inclusive, empower your teams, and maintain adaptability—i.e., don't let your settlers become so rigid that they break themselves—all while maintaining fiscally responsible oversight and a strong vision for the future.

Aha #34: What got you here won't get you there.

I got this phrase while listening to a podcast. I cannot recall which one, but apparently, there's a book with the same title by Marshall Goldsmith. I haven't read the book, but James Clear wrote this review of What Got You Here Won't Get You There.

I first heard this line from someone explaining how Moses brought the people out of slavery but didn't take them to the promised land. However, there's another biblical story that displays what I'm talking about in business transformation. King David envisioned the great temple, but he didn't build it. He was a warrior. G-d told him he could not build the temple because King David had shed blood; instead, his son Solomon, a man of peace, would build it. Warriors are conquerors who venture into new lands. They grow through acquisition, and in business, it can also be through innovation. Peace-builders create prosperity where they are.

Not only do you need two types of mindsets to grow a team—that of a nomad and a settler—but you also need to be able to switch between these mindsets as you grow through the leadership ranks.

Let the nomads move into new territory while you bring in the settlers to craft the rules for the new land.

Aha #35: When you move outside the box, *build a new box.*

You need to work outside of the box, finding new territory. Then, once you find the new territory outside of the box, you need to build a new box. Too many times, companies neglect to build the box to sustain the ground that they've conquered. It's a completely different skillset and way of thinking than what got them there.

Another history flashback: This happened when the Hellenistic Jews, who were Jews who had adopted the Greek language, "complained against the Hebraic Jews because their widows were being overlooked in the daily distribution of food" (Acts 6:1). The twelve apostles didn't want to lose momentum spreading the word of Christ to new followers (nomads), but they also recognized that the systems they had brought to recent converts (settlers) needed some governance to maintain order. So, they came together and elected seven people to govern the settlers.

"Brothers and sisters, choose seven men from among you who are known to be full of the Spirit and wisdom. We will turn this responsibility over to them and will give our attention and prayer to the ministry of the word" (Acts 1:3).

One of the challenges with scaling teams is that connected leaders need to have both the ability to lead nomads and settlers. They may have better skills in one area or another, but they have to lead both kinds of people.

Nomads are bored in established teams. They need freedom to go outside the borders. Settlers are frustrated or anxious in new teams. They need clarity and security.

Leaders at scale need to understand this. One of the first jobs for scaling is identifying those in their teams who are the advancers and those who are the stabilizers and empowering them to work collectively.

> *Taoism for the connection here! One of the most popular symbols of Taoism is the Yin and Yang, which symbolizes the interactivity of two opposing forces. Generally, it represents good and evil, but it also represents light and dark, dry and moist, aggressive and passive. In essence, to exist, we need the push-and-pull dynamic.*
>
> *The same is true for expansion and stabilization in business. You have to have both! Sometimes, you need more of one, and sometimes the other. The dots in the middle of the two teardrop halves of the Yin-Yang symbol show that you even need one within the other. Business leaders must be able to move between two different states at different times. Sometimes, that's innovation, and sometimes, that's stabilization and governance. Sometimes, when deep in one period, you need bursts of the other as reminders.*

Exercise 6: New lens

We need to constantly practice beginner's mind, where we take the lenses we gain and try them out on old information. This exercise is a simple one, but I want you to apply this lens to other opportunities in your leadership.

Go back and look at Aha #19 (always be willing, ready, and able to do the role that reports to you) with your new lens. Can you see how understanding the specifics of your direct report's job is most necessary for your stabilizers? That's because stabilizers need structure. You need to understand the structure and those rules to ensure they are followed and carried out for future team members. You also need to understand how your different specialized resources interact with each other and the terms of handoff between teams (whether written out or unspoken agreements).

On the other hand, your nomads wear many hats, and you are not expected to predict everything they might attempt. For these teams, you need to be able to make recommendations that spark their creativity.

The Mini-C-Suite

Now that you understand the Great Transformation, let's apply it to leadership at the top levels and see how it plays out in our C-suite. As a team gets larger, a new structure needs to form where the highest levels are the visionaries.

The CEO, being in charge of both the vision and the strategy, leads both the settlers and nomads. The COO leads the shift to stabilization, and the CMO leads the shift into new territory. Of course, they work together and overlap at times. It's a Yin-Yang relationship.

Are CEOs naturally more nomadic? I am not aware of any studies done in this area, but since many entrepreneurs eventually become CEOs and CEOs lead teams into new territory, it would stand to reason that they have more nomadic tendencies. This is why they need a strong governance-oriented stabilizer in the COO. Want to build that box while you get to continue to be the creative entrepreneur that got you started? Find your mini-COO. Check out Nate Bennett's Your Career Game and Riding Shotgun: The Role of the COO or Cameron Herold's The Second in Command: Unleash the Power of Your COO.

Once you understand this dynamic, you can apply it to all levels of leadership at scale. A connected leader understands that they need both visionaries and the stabilizers. They know what a CEO, CMO, and COO are, and they know how to build a mini-C-suite within their org substructures. For example, the mini-COO is the team lead dealing with the tactical day-to-day, and the mini-CEO is the team manager who's thinking about how the team is going to grow in the next year. The mini-CEO will then either do the sales and messaging or find someone who can. And the mini-COO will do the stabilizing actions.

The COO has always managed the process, but in the past, before the C-suite was what it is today, we used to have the COO, CFO, and CEO, where HR and IT, people and tools, fell under the COO or the CFO. It makes sense that the stabilizer would manage the tools, processes, and people since you need those things for sustainable systems. However, if you're going to grow, you need to be able to leverage them to bring you into your future, which is one of the reasons those roles now report directly to the CEO.

Exercise 7: Create your mini-C-suite

1. You are the entrepreneur and leader of your future (your mini-CEO). Build your organization as if you were dreaming it up for the first time.
2. Are you more naturally a stabilizer or an explorer of new territory?
3. What budget do you have to work with? Who is responsible for managing it (your mini-CFO)?
4. Who on your team will lead all the governance efforts (your mini-COO)?
5. Who on your team will lead all the innovation, sales, and external communication efforts (your mini-CMO)?
6. Who on your team is going to manage people relations and manage culture and internal change communications (your mini-CHRO)?
7. Who is going to ensure you have the best tools to be as effective as possible (your mini-CTO)?

If you are a team of one, you get to wear all these hats. If you have the luxury of having more than one person in your organization, identify where people's strengths and weaknesses are and have the right people helping you in your mini-C-suite.

The Leader Connection

Now that you have the people identified. What level are you at in the management structure above? If you're a first-line manager, your scope is focused on the now and this year. If you're a director, the questions you are tasking your team with should be able to sustain them for the next five years.

If you're going to scale your business, you need to treat it like you're the entrepreneur in the CEO role, and no matter how big or small your current organization is, set up your mini-C-suite.

The thing about the Great Transformation is that it's not a one-time experience. It's a constant cycle of change. Find new territory, build the box, and manage the box while sending nomads out to find new revenue. Boxes break. Stabilizers fix the box. Make a better box. Replace all the boxes. Send nomads outside the box. Repeat.

Connected leader moment: Of course it works this way. The entire universe works the same way. Things always change. Chaos theory suggests that creating order out of chaos requires some sort of filter or impact. Conversely, the second law of thermodynamics, the law of entropy, proves that order disintegrates over time. When left alone, natural states eventually go to disorder. A filter or impact is then needed to create order again. Rinse and repeat.

Transforming through Management Levels

With this knowledge, let's watch this journey play out as we grow through the ranks of management. When you're an individual contributor, you've got to do your job well (settler) and go above and beyond to get promoted (nomad).

What often happens is that the contributor who gets promoted into people management is the best at doing what they do. They may even train others on how to do it. Perhaps they're great at finding new ways to serve customers, or maybe they're the best machinists and can replicate parts with unparalleled precision.

However, these excellent contributors do not often make excellent people leaders. The transformation from being an individual contributor to a first-line people leader is the toughest transformation there is in leadership. It's no longer good enough to be the best at what you do; your job is to bring out the best in others. As a new manager, you're only as good as your team. If your team is succeeding, you're a success. If your team is failing, so are you.

It doesn't matter anymore if you are the best machinist and can jump in and create any part thrown your way. If your team cannot do it, your team will not survive the transition from visionary (creating the best part) to sustainable (creating the best part over and over again).

This is why that first-line manager or team lead often gets into the role of being a visionary—the brightest in their field also has to quickly learn how to be the beacon of stabilization. These skills are so contradictory in nature that the internal struggle in this transition is real.

If the person being promoted is a natural stabilizer, they then have to flip to the visionary characteristics to be able to lead the team.

Don't get me wrong. Every level has its own set of challenges because, as you have seen, different qualities and skills are needed at different levels. However, I have found that the first transition from being an individual contributor to a people leader is the toughest.

Good news! If you're already feeling that pain, it doesn't get worse! And if you're over that hurdle, you're past the worst part!

So, now we see that the person who got promoted was either a good visionary or an excellent stabilizer, and now they have to complement their qualities. This is the first-line people manager, often the team leader role.

Once people get past that first hurdle of moving from individual contributor to contributing through others, i.e., people management, they can easily get stuck in this first-line manager role if they don't understand the leader connection. That's because the things that make a first-line manager great are stabilizers.

The Leader Connection

The first-line manager role deals in the NOW. They have to be good at

- Removing obstacles.
- Training people.
- Teaching people how to do their jobs well.
- Managing workloads.
- Setting priorities.
- Setting goals, motivating the players, and holding people accountable.

These are very strong stabilizing factors. First-line managers are tactical. They are wired in the day-to-day, and it's often hard to step out of the day-to-day to see the bigger picture.

However, to move into department management (often a second-line manager), you have to bring in vision. You not only need to be looking at what your team needs today, but you need to understand what they will need tomorrow, and you have to stay ahead of it.

This is why the people best suited to make the move from first-line manager to department manager not only solve for today but also see patterns. They understand that the challenges their team members bring to them are likely replicated in some way with other members, and they are good at applying the small to the large. If they see one issue, they look at the root cause. They have a bigger impact not by solving that one tactical problem but by seeing where that solution might help others or prevent future issues.

The department manager's job is to help the first-line manager with the day-to-day while also pushing the team forward so it does not become stagnant. Some department managers get stuck in the vision and don't help their people develop.

Department managers

- Enable the team to do their job (remove roadblocks and provide coaching, tools, and training)
- Empower the team to do their job (enforce the vision and core principles, create a culture, and provide room for growth and mistakes within a controlled environment)
- Enforce the team to do their job (provide feedback and mitigate issues and risks)

Here are the key things directors do:

- Provide a vision and direction for the team aligned with the company vision and in support of the company goals
- Drive revenue and new market initiatives
- Develop leaders who can execute the vision, provide unparalleled service teams, obtain client SLAs, and deliver against revenue targets
- Foster the culture that supports the company mission and vision

If you're following along, you've found a challenge to scalability: constantly flipping between being visionary and stabilizing.

The Leader Connection

Role	Focus	New Territory Exploration / Governance balance
Individual Contributor	Now	Follows governance and explores new opportunities cautiously.
Team Lead / First-Line Manager	Now: 1-year plan	Creates and enforces governance. Ensures the team can maintain commitments on quality and quantity. Focuses on training. Balance of 20% new territory exploration / 80% governance unless it's a brand new team, in which case it's 80% new territory exploration and 20% governance. However, with time, as the new ways are institutionalized, the balance needs to move back to 20% innovation/80% governance.
Department Manager / Second-line Manager	1–2-year plan	40% new territory exploration / 60% governance
Director	5-year plan	70% new territory exploration / 30% governance
VP	10-year plan	90% new territory exploration / 10% governance

The Great Transformation

Summary: In this pivotal chapter, we uncovered the difference between leading in a small organization and a large one: agility and specialization. You want a bit of both. We identified that the Great Transformation is a constant ebb and flow between a growth and stabilizing mentality. We discussed how the C-Suite exemplifies the focus areas you should attend to in your organization, and we planned out how to build a mini-C-suite of your own. For both you and your team of leaders, we talked about the change needed to grow through the leadership ranks. We talked about how you need to lead across growth-minded teams as well as your stabilizers, recognizing that there's a time and a place for both the nomads and the stabilizers. The preceding chapters were preparing you for the rich content found in Chapter 6. If I wasn't effective in underscoring what was happening, I urge you to read it again with this new lens. Don't let my shortcomings in communication deter you from the rich content found in this chapter. Once you understand the message, your paradigm changes, and leading your teams through the different dynamics becomes clearer.

In the next few chapters, we're going to explore some of the best practices of stabilizers and what it takes to create a sustainable model as you scale your team.

Chapter 7
Sustainable Systems

"I've learned that everything in threes are balanced. So when
I consider my options, I don't put it in a pros and cons list,
I put it in buckets of three."
– Keith Bradley

Back in 2020, I was diagnosed with cancer. It was a huge wake-up call, which I see as a gift. Of course, it's easy for me to call the wake-up call a gift now that I'm on the other side of that journey, but let there be no doubt that there was a crash course in elevating my own leadership. I remember thinking at the time that I needed to take an extended leave from work for some of my treatment and that the team needed to be set up well to continue without me. I was too involved in the direction of the work and wondered what would happen to this team if I didn't come back from my leave. I spent the next three months having very tough conversations with people in an attempt to get them to grow at a super speed so that they could take over for me while I was out.

Here's the crash course for you:

Executing well is about having a system in place that works even when you are not working. Executing well is like investing. If we set the investment up correctly, it creates compound interest. If set up incorrectly, you're going to be dealing with a bunch of "break-fixes" and be charged a lot of energy.

If you're thinking that sounds lovely but don't know how to create a system that works for you even when you're not working, this is the chapter for you. You need a map. When you have a map, you can go out on autopilot and relax. When you don't have a map, you're constantly taking in new inputs and course-correcting. But with a map, you don't need to waste energy developing the course along the way. You only need to come in when things get off track.

What's our map? **Sustainable System = People + Process + Tools.**

Aha #36: People, processes, and tools are the three pillars of every operational business system.

Let's build the system with the end goal in mind. We will take the people, processes, and tools and design their functions around our objectives. We will wrap them in a culture of execution, creating a map so that the system continues to work for us when we're not working. That may make it sound easy, but it is hard work. As former U.S. Secretary of State Colin Powell says, "There are no secrets to success. It's a result of preparation, hard work, and learning from failure."

Let's get to work.

People

It boils down to this: First, you have to get the right people for the job. Then you have to keep them. But let's make that path a little clearer.

To GET the Right People → Hire Right
To KEEP the Right People → Onboard Right + Develop Right +
Engage Right

Hire Right

Hiring is critical. If you have to choose between hiring the wrong person or keeping the role open, in most cases, it's better to keep the role open. For scale, when you hire, pick the people who will help you achieve your objectives and support a culture of execution.

Aha #37: Hiring is a manager's most important job.

Hiring sets up the foundation for a successful team. If you don't have the right people for the job, you will end up either doing a poor job or not doing the job at all. If you're a good manager, you'll replace the person doing the job, but why go through all that if you didn't have to? If you want your system to work for you while you're not working, hire right the first time.

Hiring wrong is the fastest way to make you work harder. Hiring costs money, and not only is it going to cost exponentially more if you need to replace your hire, but you're going to be left cleaning up the shortcomings of your bad hire.

Bonus Material: Go to www.MintROI.com for a series on hiring right.

Onboard Right

Once you hire the right person, you don't want to lose them. That's why you have to onboard right. Many studies show that most people who quit do so within their first 90 days of employment. These studies suggest two main culprits:

1. Bad expectations set within the hiring process. The job or company fit was not aligned with the new hire's expectations.
2. Bad onboarding experience.

If hiring is the most important job of a manager, onboarding is the job managers are most likely to get wrong. According to a Gallup poll, only 12% of employees say their organization does a great job onboarding.

Aha #38: Go slow to go fast.

Remember how the momentum curve required us to go slow at the beginning to gain exponential speed later? Onboarding right has the same requirement. My map to onboarding right is that you plan for an active learning path for the first 90 days. The new hire can begin doing their actual work in week two or even week one in some cases, but don't expect them to be at full capacity until 90 days and meet their output levels at 120 days.

People often ask me which is better, classroom training or the shadow method. They both have their time and place. I'm a huge proponent of guided shadow training where there's a set of parameters, a checklist if you will, for the objectives of the training. In my experience, however, employees don't feel like they have been trained unless they have had some formal training activity such as classroom training or computer-based training. So, the best training program has a combination of both.

Have you seen the SODOTO method? It stands for "see one, do one, teach one." It was developed in the 1800s as a training program for medical students, but I have found it very useful in the first 90 days of employment. I have my new hires watch someone else. Then they do the job while someone else watches, and then they teach the job to someone (sometimes, it's the trainer, and sometimes, it's a new hire).

The "teach one" is often missed in regular shadow training, but this is where significant learning comes in. If a person knows they have to teach what they're learning, they will learn it better. Also, they will be asked questions that maybe they didn't think about, allowing them to grow their own knowledge. Give it a try. It works.

Bonus Material: Go to www.MintROI.com for a more detailed map of the onboarding journey.

Develop Right

Development requires two inputs.

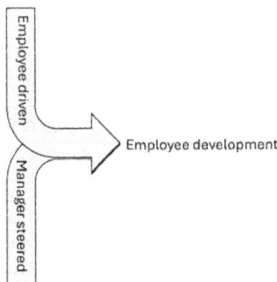

Employees need to take ownership of their development, and the manager needs to take ownership of the direction of the development.

The employees' goal for the business and their development is to actively progress toward where they want to go. The manager's goal for their employees' development should be to lead them where the business needs them. The sweet spot is when the employees' directional wants and the business's directional wants are aligned.

Remember Aha #21, that a shadow is the fastest way to create a clone? That works great in an environment where all you ever want is more of what you have, but we also know that those get stagnant and eventually die.

When developing others, give them some freedom to put their own touch on things. This will propel you into the future while you're doing something else.

Nearly two decades ago, when I was a regional manager, I had several local managers who reported to me. There was one manager in the Southwest—we will call him Ramon—who had a particularly difficult stakeholder. Ramon struggled with hitting the hiring targets he needed to achieve. Month after month, we didn't meet our numbers. It was very frustrating because before Ramon had been hired, I had stepped in as the interim manager and been able to achieve the numbers. I suspected that Ramon wasn't following my process, but he was very senior, and I had hired him to do his job, so I wanted to let him do it without micromanaging him.

During one site visit, the difficult stakeholder pulled me into her office, and my stomach just flipped with anxiety. I knew she was going to yell at me for not having met our numbers. Instead, she proceeded to tell me how my management style was all wrong and how she had just come back from a conference. She ended up giving me one of the most powerful keys to leadership that I've used for the past 20 years: situational leadership. Even then, 20 years ago, it was already very old. It was developed by leadership experts Paul Hersey and Ken Blanchard in 1969, and it came out in the book *Management of Organizational Behavior: Utilizing Human Resources*.

Here's my take on how I make it work for me.

Style Awareness Guide

Employee's Experience with Task/Job	Role of manager	Insights
New to a job	Direct/Dictate	Give them step-by-step instructions and check in often. Hold them accountable for both precision and accuracy until they have shown you that they know how to do the job.
Some experience	Coach	Guide them. Don't assume they know the right questions to ask. Tip: This phase is tricky because, sometimes, people think they are experts. They know just enough to be dangerous, so they are not always open to coaching. This is when you have to help them see where they still have opportunities for improvement.
Nearing expertise	Mentor	Be there for questions they ask, but unless they check in with you, there's no need for you to proactively check in with them. Tip: Sometimes, people hold on to your support as a crutch for a little too long. This is when you have to build up their confidence to the next level. Help them know they have this.
Expert	Delegate	Toss it over to them and forget about it. This is such a lovely place. Your goal is to have as many people in this area as possible.

A person can be new to a role but not new to every aspect of the role. They can also be a very experienced resource but get a new project that's outside of their wheelhouse, and they can find themselves new to that particular job. In that scenario, you would go back to directing mode. In each job, you cycle through these phases, but a person could be in multiple phases at once if they have different experience levels with different jobs they are doing.

Think of this as a progression path for each task or job, a stair step, if you will. For each new kind of job, you and your team member will have to scale a different set of stairs. Of course, where there is crossover, you can skip straight to the current level of competency.

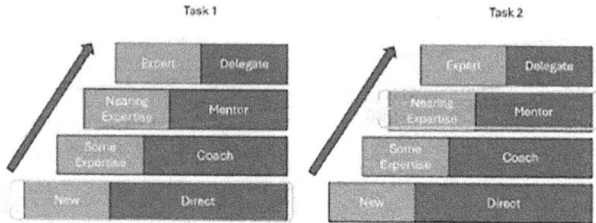

Sometimes, you can be coaching, other times delegating, and other times directing. It can be very confusing to your team and cause you to appear to be inconsistent in your leadership approach. My advice is to educate your team members on the model so they understand why your style will change with them and why you sometimes will dive in deep and other times give them space. If you're not meeting them where they are, you could risk losing their engagement.

Connected leader moment: One of my favorite authors is Maya Angelou. I adore her quotable life philosophies, like this one: "When someone shows you who they are, believe them the first time."

Here's how I apply this particular philosophy in my leadership: Until an employee has shown me they are competent in an area, I have a reason to check in on them and follow up with them. Once an employee has earned my trust, I stop inspecting. Doing so is only wasting my time and theirs. If, on the other hand, an employee has given me reason not to trust them, I will dive in deep and validate their work with a much more critical eye until they have redeemed that trust. Trust the first time is easy to obtain, but once that trust is broken, it's much harder to regain.

The Leader Connection

Engage Right

Gallup defines employee engagement as the involvement and enthusiasm of employees in the workplace. If employee retention is the objective, employee engagement is a KPI, a key indicator of performance—in this case, the performance of whether we are going to retain that employee. As said previously, you want to reduce the effort it takes to hire new employees by hiring right and retaining the right people.

Engagement is about providing work that excites people, educating them on how to do the work, giving them the freedom to make decisions, and setting up a reward system that keeps them motivated. I have an equation for maximizing engagement.

Exciting work + Empowerment + Motivation = Engaged Employees

Let's break down each of those elements:

Motivation = Various Fuels

We covered the fuel that drives the team in Chapter 4. Let me add that, sometimes, businesses think they make motivation easy when they plan out their rewards program, often using compensation and benefits as the reward. Money is a common motivator because it can be used to buy other things. But buyer beware! This motivation technique isn't a one-size-fits-all. Sometimes, people see compensation as a given for them to be in the job, and it no longer holds a reward value for them once they have obtained the job. They need something new. Each person is motivated differently. As a manager, it's your job to understand what motivates your team members and to set up opportunities for them to feel rewarded.

Exciting work = Work + A Compelling Reason
for That Person to Want to Do the Work

If a person is not intrinsically excited about the work, it's a manager's job to help them see how the work can be exciting. Every job can be exciting for someone. It's about the frame of the story. Is there an opportunity? Will this lead to something? If you need to, go back to Chapter 2 and think about perspective, connection, and application.

Empowerment = Freedom to Act + Education

Creating a safe environment where you can grow from failure is the only way I know how to give people the freedom to act. If you show me a manager who constantly corrects everything the team does and needs all the decisions to be run through him or her, I'll show you a team that doesn't do much on its own. But it's not enough to give people the freedom to fail; you also have to give them the tools to succeed. This is where education paired with freedom to act is so critical. We covered one kind of education when we talked about onboarding. Another path to empowerment is through open and 360-degree communication.

There are going to be times when you cannot be there to guide everything. You can prepare your team for those times by showing them your expectations, wrapping them into basic principles, and letting them swim. Give them stretch assignments. This is how people grow at speed.

Aha #39: Leaders aren't born; they're made.

Time and time again, the best leaders navigate through the most difficult times. They are not coddled. The old saying that a diamond is formed through pressure holds true here. Giving your team stretch assignments helps develop leaders on your team and helps you be able to do more with less.

When you give your team stretch assignments, avoid the urge to dictate or delegate. It's best if you toggle between coach and mentor, depending on what your employee needs from you.

Exercise 8: Team assessment

Let's do a really good assessment of your team right now.

1. First, what are all the different roles on your team?
2. How many different people do you have doing the same role?
3. Now, what does it look like in that role? Write up your job description. Don't use the job descriptions you've been given. Let's start over.
4. When writing a job description, let's begin with the end in mind. What are the outputs of the job?
5. What does good look like? Think about the people who are doing this job particularly well and what makes them better than the others.
6. Now, what competencies do you need?
7. Do you have the skills you need?

This is what you're looking for. The above things will help you understand your minimal requirements.

8. Would you be willing to make exceptions on those? If you had a stellar candidate, what skills or competencies would you be willing to give in on?

For any requirements you said you could be flexible with, even though you think they are requirements, they are not requirements. They are the assets that you'd like to have. Requirements are things you are not willing to give on, no matter how stellar the candidate is.

9. Now, how does your team measure up against your requirements and like-to-haves?
   a. Who is meeting all the requirements?
   b. Who is bringing in some like-to-haves?
10. What can you do to develop those people to level them up to BOTH your requirements and your like-to-haves?

11. What gaps do you have on your team?

What did we say you need to do when you don't have all the skills that you need on your team? You must build, buy, or outsource.

If the gap is something you will need long-term and you have time to develop talent within, build. Grow the skillset within your team.

If the gap is something you need long term, but you need it fast, buy. Hire externally. That will also allow you more time to continue to build more talent within.

If the gap is short-term or not in your team's core responsibility set, outsource. Get a partner vendor or a contractor who has already grown through trial and error and has a nice set of tools to bring to the table that might otherwise take you months or years to develop internally.

When you did Exercise #8, you may have identified some people who are meeting all your requirements but haven't made it to the exemplary group yet. Develop them.

Process

Start with the people. When a process is designed to support the people, it does one of two things.

- Give people direction so you don't have to
- Provides governance to ensure the people are staying on course

If you want to create a culture of execution, all processes should be KISSed: keep it simple, stupid. Hey, it's not my saying, and I don't like calling people stupid, but it's good to know that overcomplicating things is a little bit stupid. All things should have a simple end-user solution.

Sometimes, however, to get to the simple user interface, you have to have layers of complexity underneath. That's where process guides come in.

Aha #40: Organization is key to getting ahead. Simplification is the key to people using it.

Process Guides

Process guides are maps to success. Cooks and bakers have recipes, explorers have maps, governments have laws, religions have doctrines, scientists have procedures, and doctors have logs.

Process guides are important tools for knowledge workers and physical laborers alike. Process guides often come in all shapes and sizes, including instruction manuals, operations manuals, process maps, checklists, and standard operating procedures (SOPs). The more judgment a role requires, the less prescriptive the process guide needs to be. For this reason, process guides are most commonly used at the first-line level, and my thoughts on this pertain to how to set up the front lines for success.

One of the most common mistakes at the front-line level that I see is inconsistent quality and performance because the process is not clearly documented. Documentation is used in businesses like macros are with computers. Macros record a process step by step, and then they take the time to set it up, but once they're set up, they can replicate actions over and over again because the system knows what it's supposed to do.

Documented processes also allow for direction to sink in. How many times have you said something to someone and then come back to find that the person doesn't recall the conversation? It's not enough that you've said it. They have to have the mindset to hear what you're saying. Having something in writing that an employee can refer back to when you're not talking helps.

Do not expect detailed guides to be used after the initial training purpose. Once people are done learning the content, they don't refer back to it. If you need them to, then you need to make it a simple one-page reference guide they can easily access.

So, why do all the detailed versions at all?

- Training: They are a spectacular training tool, setting very clear expectations.
- Governance: If the details matter, they provide a contract between the employee and the manager on the expectations of the task.
- Alignment: Getting the guide clear at the detail level means there's no question on who is doing what.

There's an added benefit to process documents in that they are like a set of laws. If a patrol officer pulls over a person for speeding, the officer can say, "It's not me; it's the law." In this way, the manager has a document to point at, taking the emotion, opinions, and charge out of a potentially difficult conversation.

I tell people that operations manuals and SOPs are outdated the moment they're created. Never print any of the detailed versions of these because you will have people following outdated processes. It's okay to print one-pagers and checklists.

Type of Content	Example	Medium
Detailed	SOP, process guide	Digital (don't print)
High Level	Checklist, one-pager	Handout or tangible reference guide

- Keep the document simple.
- Keep the storage mechanism simple.

- Perform quarterly or annual reviews for accuracy.

If this is not your forte, it's okay. Remember: you found your mini-COO, so give this job to them.

Governance

Another thing your mini-COO should own is the governance cadence. Governance includes both accountability and communication.

If your process document outlines your expectations, what are you going to do to ensure people are following them? After all, a set of words are just words. From a process perspective, they are meaningless if they're not turned into behaviors.

Communication is how you circulate the behaviors you want. Accountability is how you ensure your team is doing the right behaviors.

Communication + Holding People Accountable → Right Behaviors

Communication Cadence
Group Meetings

Leader	Meeting	Frequency	Mode
Team leads / first-line managers	Team meeting	Weekly	Informal with open dialogue
Department manager	Department meeting	Monthly	Slightly more formal and may have some dialogue but more presentation
Business unit leaders (directors or VPs)	Town hall	Quarterly	Most formal with the least dialogue

Sustainable Systems

You're not the center of the universe, but you are the center of your universe, and the people who come into contact with you can make or break your initiatives. Wouldn't you want to engage them in such a way that you're aligned and working together?

One-to-Ones (For Managers with Roughly Ten Direct Reports)

Who	Cadence
Direct Reports	Weekly or semi-weekly
Peers	Monthly
Up/down one level	Quarterly
Up/down two levels	Annually

These charts are meant for managers with a team of approximately ten direct reports. I've seen managers with over a hundred direct reports where most of their efforts go to being an HR resource vs. an operational manager. I've also seen managers with one to two direct reports who have individual contributor responsibilities. The sweet spot seems to be that managers who are also individual contributors tend to be able to handle from one to five employees. Managers who don't have individual contributor responsibilities tend to be able to manage seven to 15 employees, with ten being optimal.

Of course, the exact number varies, and there are many factors to consider with ideal team sizes. If you have more or fewer direct reports, your meeting cadence will likely need to adjust accordingly.

Accountability:

Performance reviews are designed to hold people accountable for their goals. However, all too often, performance reviews are on an annual cycle. I don't believe accountability can wait. It's something that must be built into a regular feedback cycle, preferably in your regular one-to-ones. I tell my team that performance reviews should be boring because there shouldn't be any surprises.

Some jobs have a clear line of sight to accountability guidelines. For instance, there might be a quality control measurement with a certain expectation for a defect-free product or service. However, in many knowledge-worker roles, the measurement of success is less clear. If you are familiar with SMART goals, you know that goals should be measurable. This is how you know whether or not you are achieving those goals, and it's by that measurement that we can hold people accountable.

Remember Aha #23 and #24. This is a good place to combine them. What can you measure to ensure the highest amount of accountability? Hint: it's not quantity; it's quality. These are things like customer satisfaction and anything that will increase your credibility with a customer. Referrals are still one of the highest rates of return. People who don't yet know you trust what even strangers will tell them.

Tools

The final pillar of a sustainable system is tools. Technically, process guides are the tools that describe a process, but I put them in the process section because, while I don't know your process, I know the process tools that can help you succeed.

What other tools do you need to succeed? Presumably, technology came to mind. Of course, specifically, it's software tools. Software is constantly changing, and I don't pretend to be an expert on all the optimization and automation tools available. So, we are not going to spend time here discussing different software technologies. It'll be outdated the moment this is published.

When you are thinking about your tools, software is not the only tool to consider. Also consider:

Sustainable Systems

- Hardware, such as computers and accessories.
- Facilities, such as desks and chairs.
- Office supplies.

You're a connected leader. Here's my advice. Either tools can support the process, or the process can support the tools. Make sure that the tools support the process so the process can support the people. When you build the process to support the tool, the people generally suffer.

Connected leader moment: I have a second bit of advice that's only recently become more apparent to me. Throughout time, technology was built to help people do more, but somewhere along the way, someone thought that it meant we'd have more free time to use as we like. It doesn't. We will always fill the space with something. Make sure it's the right thing. From the invention of fire to industrialization, computers, and now AI, this trend has held true. The time that those tools saved didn't help us relax more; it helped us do more. Don't forget this. Get back to your Eisenhower Matrix and identify the most important things you should be doing. When your tools create space, fill it with the important things, not just more stuff.

And there you have it. I've just given you my recipe for building a sustainable system. It's up to you to execute. Execute well.

The Leader Connection

Summary: This chapter details the recipe for building sustainable teams:

Hire Right + Onboard Right + Develop Right + Engage Right

These skills are particularly challenging for growth-minded nomads who are traditionally focused on results but don't want to be bogged down with the details. For each of the elements above, I provided some supporting guidance for building sustainable teams. Settlers and stabilizers, beware: there's a caution for you, too. Remember not to get mired in governance, or else you will sink the ship. As I mentioned in Chapter 6, to scale sustainably, you need both the flexibility of the explorers and the nomads, along with the stability and governance that the settlers bring.

Chapter 8
At Scale

"Give me a lever long enough and a fulcrum on which to place it,
and I shall move the world."
– Archimedes

Everyone's world is the same size. You may manage no one, and John may manage a team of five hundred, but John's world is no bigger than yours. You can both fit only so much into 24 hours. You both journey around the sun together and arrive at the same spot at the same time. You both put your pants on one leg at a time. As humans, we can only keep so much going at the same time. Feelings like pain, stress, and joy are universal, but their intensity changes with perspective.

Think back to your first job interview. Remember how nervous you felt? Can you recall the pressure you put on yourself? Do you remember how confusing those first few days were? I'll bet doing the exact same thing all over again now would be a breeze. You'd know what to expect, and you'd have a different perspective.

Perspective is everything. It's the changing force. Time is relative. Speed is relative. Knowledge is relative. You can make little leaps within your current construct, but to make truly large jumps, you must change your perspective. What you focus on is the perspective you choose to take. Tim Cook, the CEO of Apple, said, "You can focus on things that are barriers, or you can focus on scaling the wall or redefining the problem." It's a great reminder to approach challenges with a solution-oriented mindset.

Aha #41: Reframe the problem.

Cook has given us another tool in reframing the problem. Problems are not walls to scale but opportunities to grow. We can hate that the project got derailed by an unexpected turn of events, or we can say we expected something unexpected would come up—here it is; I've found you now, and now I'm one step closer to completing the project.

Reframing the problem allows us to handle things that, at first, appear to be outside our control. Albert Einstein once said, "If I had an hour to solve a problem...I'd spend the first 55 minutes determining the proper questions to ask, for once I know the proper question, I can solve the problem in less than five minutes." When we focus on ensuring we have the perspective first, we're ensuring we're asking the right questions to solve the right problem.

Often, what we think is the problem is only a symptom of the underlying problem. When we address the symptoms, the issue still arises elsewhere. So, if we spend a little more time ensuring we are solving the right challenges, we will spend less time revisiting those same challenges.

Aha #42: Don't work in a vacuum.

Within your organization, you will have interconnected jobs. Identify the interconnected points and make sure they can communicate to each other what they are doing. Effective communication, I've learned, requires communicating early and often, and it often means repetition. The more important the message is, the more you need to repeat it in different ways so that it is heard. Not all people will receive your message and will be in a place to understand it when you first present it, so be ready to share it more than once.

You also need to share the message with more than just the people you're likely thinking about. You need to share it with the end users, too. Just as 360-degree communication is important at a leader level, it's important at a department level, too. Treat your department like it was a person; if something new is happening, discuss it with all the stakeholders who are impacted and get their feedback and input.

Now, I can see some of you saying, "But Shanda, if I did this on everything, I would be in constant communications, and if I waited on everyone to provide feedback, nothing would change."

Bingo!

Stabilizers listen up! There's a reason the chapter on execution comes before this one. History shows us that leaders who succeed in their objectives have consistently prioritized execution before perfection. You have to be able to make swift decisions. You have to take all the inputs you receive, but you are the ultimate decision-maker because only you are the mini-CEO of your organization. Your stakeholders should provide influence, but you are in control. So, as a CEO, you should know how critical the decisions will be in your organization and how quickly they need to be made. This tells you who should be making the decision and how many inputs you need for an informed decision to be made.

Being the best in your business means owning or influencing as many of the factors in your business as you can.

Over the years, I've been accused of growing an empire. This is because I tend to start with one book of business in my remit and slowly but surely expand my remit into related areas. It's also because everything is interrelated. When I own responsibility for one part of the business, I often need support from another part of the business. If the support is not up to the level that I need it to be, I help them to be successful, not by controlling them but by being an effective customer.

If I were a winemaker, I'd want the wine to taste good. I'd need to ensure the vine was well watered, getting lots of sunshine, and was pest-free. That's all within my control if I own the vineyard. But the vineyard is not enough for good wine. I'd need to think about the barrels that I age the wine in and the flavor the different barrel types bring. In this scenario, the vine is my responsibility, and the barrels are not, but they certainly should be within my influence so I can have the best wine possible. So, as the buyer of the barrel, I would select the best. If I only had one vendor to work with, I would provide feedback on my needs. If the vendor didn't change their ways, I would think about the buy, build, or outsource model described in Chapter 5.

When outsourcing isn't working, you buy or build. But watch me now: if you're going to buy or build, you're moving into new territory. You're thinking outside your box. So, now you'll have to build a new box and use all the tools in your toolkits to build that sustainable system.

I had an employee who could outperform any of her peers. When I analyzed what she was doing differently, I realized that she was curious and not afraid to overstep. This is what made her a great individual contributor. But her work wasn't replicable. She didn't build the box, and when she moved to her next job, no one behind her could recreate what she did. My point is that before you optimize, you have to build your sustainable baseline.

Optimizing something that never worked well to begin with is like cutting the leg off a two-legged stool. Build the foundation before constructing the foundation at scale. All too often, business leaders move on to the next best thing before they've stabilized what they've created. Sometimes, this occurs because they see the next best thing clearly but don't see the instability of the place they are leaving behind.

Bezos and Zen

Jeff Bezos famously wrote letters to his shareholders. His 1997 letter has been the most quoted. It's known as "The Day 1 Letter." In it, Bezos says there's a long road ahead, but this is Day 1, where the focus is on the future. Now, Amazon was founded in 1994, but in 1997, it went public. Every year since then, Bezos has attached a copy of his original 1997 letter to the shareholders, which says, "This is Day 1 for the internet, and if we execute well, for Amazon.com." In the letter, he speaks about the principles of execution that have since become part of the culture of Amazon.com: maintaining long-term focus, obsessing over customers, and boldly innovating. He's also changing their perspective. It's not Day 10,673; it's Day 1.

By starting over with fresh eyes every day, you see more things than if you kept the status quo.

Throwback to the Buddhist practice of beginner's mind that we mentioned in Chapter 2.

Sometimes, seeing a challenge at work with fresh eyes is all it takes to realize the answer was right in front of you all along. But when we are mired in the day-to-day, it isn't easy to do this. Try this little thought exercise. Close your eyes. Pretend you know nothing and wipe your mind clean. Forget you know the words for common things like "tree" and "chair." When you open your eyes, look around you as if you were seeing the area you're in for the very first time. Notice curiosity taking over and the vibrant possibility of the world around you. That's a glimpse of the beginner's mind.

Now imagine doing that with your organization. That's what Bezos gives us by asking us to treat every day like it's Day 1. There are obstacles to overcome, sure, but the possibilities are endless. Isn't that just a little bit motivating?

Ready for more tools in your toolkit? We're going to add a few that will help enable you to look at your organization with a beginner's mind: Six Sigma, Lean Sigma, Agile, and Scrum. You don't have to be formally trained in these methods to be able to draw connections from their application.

Six Sigma, Lean, Agile, and Scrum

Back in the '90s, Six Sigma became a popular optimization technique among manufacturing firms. Motorola came out with the concept and registered it as a service in 1991. Manufacturing and engineering companies like Honeywell and General Electric were quick to become early adopters.

The concept was that by reducing variations, you could improve the process, products, and services. Soon, everyone was jumping on the bandwagon, with some estimates being that two-thirds of Fortune 500 company corporations had Six Sigma initiatives by the end of the decade.

In the early 2000s, everyone jumped to Lean, which was Six Sigma with a lean or wasteless twist. The Lean movement found success outside manufacturing, but it was rigid and couldn't flex with the dynamics of the business.

Then came Agile and Scrum, which adapted to business challenges and were much more flexible. Because of their flexibility, they took off in human-centric services and software industries.

We can learn from this when thinking about business at scale. When scaling a business, you have to do the work to identify the right processes (Six Sigma), find the cheapest and fastest way (Lean), change based on needs (Agile), and continuously improve (Scrum).

Exercise 9: Where should you focus first: Six Sigma, Lean, Agile, or Scrum against time, money, and people?

Rate these statements on a scale of one to five, with one being least accurate and five being most accurate:

1. My business processes are clearly articulated.
2. Everyone in my organization understands their purpose and the purpose of the teams they work with.
3. My business has repeatable processes that don't change often.
4. Quality control is under control.

5. My processes are updated.

For anything that was rated a three or below, you will need to do some clean-up. Start with the lowest-scoring opportunity. The key below will help you identify which tool to use with the scenario corresponding to each of the above statements.

1. Six Sigma
2. Six Sigma
3. Six Sigma, Lean, or Agile (or a combination). If your business requires customizability more than standardization, start with an Agile-first approach.
4. Lean Sigma
5. Scrum

It's basic housekeeping. We already know that over time, order eventually moves back to chaos. We've got to come back in and keep it cleaned up.

Let's look at some ways to optimize your resources, creating the longest lever possible for sustainable systems: time, money, and people.

If

Sustainable System = People + Process + Tools

Then

Sustainable System at Scale = (People + Process + Tools) x (Leverage)

At Scale

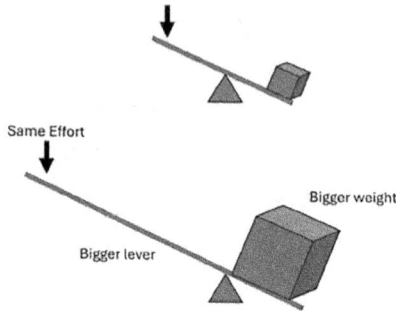

For bigger change, use more leverage.

A company's resources are time, money, and people. If these are what you have available to use as leverage, are you optimizing all of them?

Time

Time is a finite resource. You'll never get more of it. Therefore, you want to maximize the efficiency of how you spend your time.

Science connection: Connecting time and energy concepts. The law of perpetual transmission of energy states that energy is constantly moving. Time seemingly works like this. I say seemingly because, as Einstein proved, time is relative. However, in our world and from our perspective, time seems to constantly progress forward. Energy is never stagnant. We also know that larger objects have more energy. If we know that the law of perpetual transmission of energy says that energy is going to flow through whatever forces act within it, then what if the space we fill our time with does the same thing?

What if whatever we fill our time up with is giving or taking our energy? And what if larger mental items, or things that are more consuming, have more energy in the same way that larger physical items do? We know that the bigger the challenge, the more drained we feel.

So, if we can see that these two situations are acting in similar ways, is there a pattern we can pull from in our knowledge of how energy flows that we can then apply to our business to help us stay optimized without burnout? You are the connector. I'd love to hear from you at www.MintROI.com.

Yes, we're talking about your time, but we're also talking about the time of your entire organization.

To be clear, maximizing the efficiency of your time does not mean filling your time to the max with activities. That's a waste of time. Maximizing efficiency requires choosing activities wisely to maximize the result of the time you have. Select highly rewarding activities.

I assume most of you have seen the popular clip where a professor has a jar, some big rocks, some pebbles, and some sand. If you start by putting the sand and the pebbles in the jar first, you won't have room for the big rocks. The trick is to start with the big rocks first, then the pebbles, and finally the sand. This is true for the activities you choose to fill your time with. Start with the big activities and then sprinkle in the smaller ones where you have available space. The key here is to schedule the important big blocks first.

Why waste your time on anything that is not important? If the block, whether big or small, is not important to you or others, get rid of it. This is much easier said than done, especially when everything seems important. If you are unsure of what is important, the item with the highest impact is the most important.

If it's important to others but not as important to you, you can delegate it.

It's all relative, right? Importance is a value we place on things. Something can be unimportant to you but valuable to someone else. This could be an opportunity for delegation. Let's not forget the value of giving someone an opportunity to have a new experience.

Aha #43: Wasting time is an expense. Wasting a lot of time is a huge expense.

If time is money, wasting time is throwing away money. Use your time for the highest-reward activities. This is why people with the best judgment should be making the most critical decisions. They don't have to make many decisions. In fact, they shouldn't be making many decisions because you want their time spent thinking about the different dynamics of the few critical decisions they have to make. I created the image below from ideas that originated in *The Almanack of Naval Ravikant: A Guide to Wealth and Happiness* by Eric Jorgenson. The higher the impact of the decision is, the more judgment you need to make and the more processing time you should allow for it. Your less experienced resources should be making many decisions on lower-impact items.

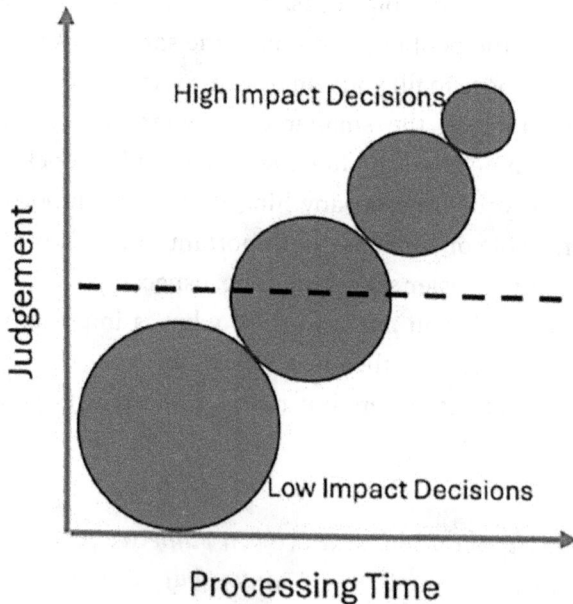

Experience is relative. Everyone at the same age has the same amount of experience but in different things. Therefore, someone with less experience than you in running your organization would not have the same level of opportunity to sharpen their judgment for decisions within your organization if your organization is the same as it was in the past. However, that same person has, by definition, more experience than you outside of the things you've experienced. Isn't it possible that they may have a perspective you could benefit from?

For this group of individuals, you create a safe environment to make informed decisions so they can recover from their decision if they don't choose the best outcome. This group of people includes your future big decision-makers. Give them a chance to practice and sharpen their skills on the small things.

Your big blocks should be spent thinking about the biggest challenges that only you, with your experience, can solve. You don't need to solve anything alone. You're experienced; you know people.

Throwback moment to Aha #18: Knowledge is of two kinds, that of which you already know and knowing where to find what you don't know.

You should fill your space with things that will support your ability to manage the big blocks in the future.

Remember Aha #24: Focus on the one thing. As Keller & Papasan say, find the one thing that, when you do it, all other things fall into place.

When you have time to spare, a wise way to use your time is to fill your space with things that make your big blocks in the future smaller blocks. As we learned in Chapter 4, these are things that create potential energy and include activities such as 1) coming up with new ideas to increase revenue or decrease costs and 2) learning. Self-improvement is always a fuel for potential energy. Encourage your employees to do the same by teaching them the principles of big and small blocks, not by planning their time for them. Few things are more demotivating than micromanaging employees' time.

Throwback moment to Chapter 4, where we learned that motivation equals energy and energy pointed right is directly proportional to income. Therefore, demotivation has a direct relationship with losing money or potential energy.

If you're looking for an employee to fill up every moment, believe me, they will not disappoint, but they're not going to fill up their time with big blocks. Knowledge workers are hired for their judgment, and this includes judgment on how to use their time wisely. If you take away that judgment autonomy, you are disabling their potential.

People will use their time to the minute when they are watched to the minute, but they will fill it with the less important things and waste their time and yours. This is why watching the clock and waiting until 5 p.m. to make sure that your employee doesn't leave a minute before five is not only fruitless but detrimental. Your employee knows you're watching them do this, and so they're going to be filling up their time with the little blocks.

Aha #44: Delegate the right thing at the right time to the right person.

When done right, delegating has the potential to exponentially create "leave it and forget about it" systems, just as investing allows for compound interest while you're sleeping. The trick is to delegate the right thing at the right time to the right person.

Until you're at that point where you have the right thing, the right person to delegate to, and the right time to delegate it, my advice would be not to leave it and forget about it. It's like an investor. You have to do a lot of research to minimize your downside because, when you delegate the wrong thing to someone, you're taking a huge risk. When you delegate to the wrong someone, you're also taking a huge risk. Until you've confirmed you have the right thing with the right person at the right time, you haven't delegated correctly.

Aha #45: 80 is the new 100.

Have you ever heard of the 80/20 rule? There are so many things that this rule works for. Often, 80% of the time goes to 20% of the problems, but if you're working on solving a group of problems, ensure you're solving for the 80%, not the 20%.

When my team comes in to consult on business improvements on process, we often coordinate focus groups and run through existing processes with the experts who are entrenched in the day-to-day of the job. These people too often think of all the things that could go wrong in a process, and they try to solve every possible scenario because they've seen it. They don't realize that by doing this, they're reducing the opportunity for the bulk of the work to flow smoothly 80% of the time. They're focused on the 20% of the time in which issues can arise, and believe me, they never cover 100% of the issues that could arise. It's a huge waste of time.

Here are a few 80/20s that I have found to work at least 80% of the time:

- 20% of the problems can cause 80% more work.
- 80% of the problems can only take 20% of the work.
- 80% of the work year can go toward output production. The other 20% of the work year goes toward sick leave, vacation time, training, and administrative duties.
- When calculating max outputs, only use 80% of the time as production time.

- Bezos had a rule about making decisions when you have 70% of the inputs.
- 80% done well is better than 100% done perfectly. Perfect never gets done. Or, in our terms today, done is better than perfect.

To find out why this works, read The 80/20 Principle *by Richard Koch.*

Priorities and Distractions

When you identify your big block items, these should be your priorities. But if you don't give enough time to completing a priority task, you're creating switch tasks, leaving gaps for more distractions when you switch back and forth between varying priorities. The people who are seemingly good at multitasking are, in reality, good at switch-tasking. Unfortunately, efficiency is lost as you switch tasks, and the more tasks you switch between increases that loss.

We have created many tools to help us be more efficient, but they ended up causing more distractions (email, texts, inner-office messaging systems, social media platforms, and the list goes on). In the case of email, it can be a great tool to tag an item that needs to be completed later, but in doing so, we see ten new items that require our attention.

Throwback moment to the energy section where we identified that momentum is a multiplier at scale. One of those reasons was that you didn't have to overcome inertia. When you are switch-tasking, you lose momentum and are constantly using energy to overcome inertia.

When you have too many things going on, you rush from one thing to the next without completing anything. It's the opposite of exponential; it's de-potential. You can't get your most important tasks done. Then you're stretched too thin. You may stop resting. Things don't go well.

Sometimes, this is by unconscious effort—your time goes to whatever is getting your attention at the moment. You attend to the wheel that is squeaking. But sometimes, your time goes to whatever you are most comfortable with. If, for instance, you have a big job that you don't know how you will succeed at and a small job that you've done a million times, you're more likely to knock out the small job, and the big job doesn't budge.

To get back on track, you need to minimize distractions and opportunities for distractions. In some cases, this means putting enough time aside to complete a task, even if that means scheduling more time than you think you may need.

Aha #46: Sometimes, the best distraction mitigation is elimination (minimization).

"Busy is a sign of your life getting out of control."
– Derek Sivers, TED speaker, author, and CD Baby founder.

Remember that neither matter nor energy can be created or destroyed, but it can be transformed. The same is true with your time. If you're not focused on the right things, your time simply goes to the wrong things. It transforms into something else. I know this is obvious once stated, but it's not so obvious when you're giving your time to things that give you high dopamine rewards in the short term without giving you high-value returns in the long term.

My grandmother used to say, "Too much of anything, no matter how good it is, is good for nothing." If you find yourself with too many priorities, go back to Aha #24. What one thing would help you remove other things? It's really hard to juggle all the things you have to know. If you can, focus on getting great at one at a time. If you cannot afford that luxury, be prepared for the journey to take a little bit longer as you lose momentum switching between tasks.

Money

In any for-profit business, the goal is to make money. Money is the ticket to all your resources. It's also a resource that can be used in different ways to create leverage. You want the biggest margin. To make it easy, we'll call this profit.

Revenue - Expenses = Profit

To get more profit, you can either increase your revenue or decrease your expenses.

You can spend money on your resources to increase revenue or reduce expenses. For instance, an investment in education makes a stronger workforce that is more agile. An investment in technology can create optimization. I assume this is all obvious and won't spend much of your time discussing it. What's important to remember is that you need to watch how your money is working for you. When it's not working, move it to something that is. You need to watch it as you would your personal finances. If you have a large sum sitting in a non-interest account, you would recognize that you need to put it in a higher-yield account, or if you have a high-interest credit card that carries over a large balance, you would recognize that the fees you spend eat at your capital.

Warren Buffett, the chairman and CEO of Berkshire Hathaway, said, "Rule No. 1: Never lose money. Rule No. 2: Never forget Rule No. 1." He's speaking of investing and looking at the downside. The same is true for business. Your business is an investment. You must spend money to make money, but you need to watch out for the downside of that spend. Spending money is only an investment if it returns more capital. If it doesn't, it's just a cost (expense). The way to follow the money is to create a profit and loss statement (P&L).

Every leader should be managing their P&L front and center. Sure, some leaders will intentionally manage short-term losses for long-term gains, but there's always a strategy based on finances. Without it, any conversation about scale is irrelevant. In any for-profit business, when you run out of money or potential for money, you run out of leverage. As the mini-CEO of your organization, do you have a good handle on your budget?

Bonus Material: See www.MintROI.com for additional insights on building & managing your P&L, even if you don't officially own P&L responsibilities.

This knowledge is powerful because if you can show a clear line of sight to increasing your profitability, you are creating leverage in potential money. Even if you don't have the money in hand, this leverage is a key to opening the door to get the investments your boss or investors need to make in you to scale your business.

As the mini-CFO of your organization, you need to create your own P&L and understand what leverage you can pull in order to gain additional money. This is going to be magical when you're making new arguments to fund new investments to go out into the new territory.

In his book *Zero to One*, Peter Thiel, former CEO of PayPal, said, "The value of business today is the sum of all the money it will make in the future." Thiel points out that your value is not just about the capital you have in the bank today; it's also about your potential for capital. The name of the game is increased potential for capital. For this reason, some companies are okay with taking a smaller profit now with the expectation that they will make a larger profit in the future.

Another throwback to kinetic and potential energy:
The money you have today is your kinetic energy.
The money you will make in the future is your potential energy.

People

We're back to people! Notice a trend? We said that the 3 pillars of a sustainable solution are people, processes, and tools, where the processes support the people and the tools support the people and process. We said that three key levers to scale sustainable solutions are time, money, and people (a company's resources). People are both the term and the multiplier (leverage). Often, they are the variable, too. It's no wonder we should be paying a lot of attention to our people.

Human capital is often your most expensive cost. Thus, when cutting costs, companies often look at cutting people. To avoid a situation where you have to cut team members, you should always look to maximize the efficiency of your team.

What is **maximum efficiency**? It's where a high volume of productivity can be maintained over a long period without burnout. Think of it like a marathon, not a sprint. In a sprint, you have to run as fast as you can and leave no energy reserves behind. You cannot maintain a sprint. For a marathon, you have to pace yourself all the way to the finish line. Go above maximum efficiency, and you'll run dry; drop below it, and you're leaving opportunity on the table.

Too much push can cause team burnout. Too little can cause waste. When either of these scenarios happens, you risk ruining your resource. I've only found two things that fixed this:

1. Time and incentives
2. Replacement

Notice how I said both time and incentives? When you've over- or under-fueled an employee, it costs you double to recover. Ouch. That was a costly mistake that the manager just made. And don't get me started on the cost of replacing employees: time to hire, time to train, and time to build back an optimal level of productivity.

Finding team members' maximum efficiency numbers will help you not only save time and money but will also save your resources in the long run.

Aha #47: Activities and output are in an inverse parabolic relationship.

I call this the Theory of Maximum Efficiency.

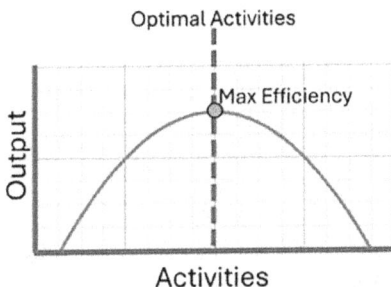

The highest sustainable output possible is the maximum efficiency number. If you have too few activities, you will not obtain the maximum efficiency number. However, what is not commonly known is that if you have too many activities, you're also not going to obtain the maximum efficiency number.

I discovered this many years ago when I was setting goals. Some people needed more work to reach their goals, but if I gave them too much, even my best employees who had reached their goals previously couldn't reach them with the increased workload. This is because they were trying to divide all their time across all their activities and not giving any single activity enough energy to complete.

I learned that if I found the right balance of workload and then withheld assigning more work until the team had the space for that work, they were more productive than if I gave them all the work at once. Now, this is tricky because some people are more productive than others and work well when they know they have more work in the pipeline. Some teams may have a stable maximum efficiency number, and others may have individual maximum efficiency numbers. In some teams, the maximum efficiency number changes because the variables change.

I assume that all work has a maximum efficiency number at any one moment.

Caution! My theory of maximum efficiency is something I've observed and even experimented on, but it's not a scientifically proven law. We know that science experiments will get the same results when all the factors are the same, but work doesn't work like that, does it? Variables must be accounted for.

If I'm selling disaster recovery solutions to a region that's hit with a lot of disasters, there's going to be a lot more need than in a more protected area. The same effort across the two regions doesn't produce the same results. The effort required had nothing to do with the input level. Thus, someone's max efficiency in one region could be higher with lower effort than someone's in another region.

Even if you have too many variables to assess a true maximum efficiency number, if you understand the concept at the core, you will be a better manager. There's a point of diminishing returns when you cover too many activities at once.

When trying to find your team's maximum efficiency level, keep the 80/20 rule in mind. An employee is fully utilized when 80% of their annual work hours are reached. I know this is going to cause some concern, so let me explain.

Let's say you offer two weeks of vacation plus two more weeks of holidays. This is low, but we'll start here. That's four weeks in total. Let's say you also allow five days of sick time (this includes doctor visits). You're at five weeks of 52 weeks a year, roughly 10% of the year, in away time. These aren't working hours, but when annual salary is based on 2,080 hours/year, they are accounted for in that calculation (40 hours/week x 52 weeks/year = 2,080 "working" hours/year. Annual salary is hourly pay x 2,080 hours).

Now let's look at actual working hours. You can expect at least one hour per week to go to meetings, one hour spent on clean-up, rework, or on random projects, and two hours a week to go to administrative tasks. That's four hours a week. In a standard 40-hour workweek, that's 10%. Add the two types of non-productive times together, and you get 20% nonproductivity—or 80% productivity. I call this 20% the rainy-day fund, and I always set it aside when I'm calculating utilization so I don't wipe out my team when the rain comes.

That rainy-day fund doesn't even account for learning curve ramp-ups. There's a learning curve at the beginning of any job. Learning is hard on people, and it takes effort. So, with newbies, you have to account for the effort of the learning curve.

However, once they get past that learning curve, you can't ease up or else they're going to get lazy. So, when you start slow to help with the learning curve, you're going to have to add responsibility as the employee continues to progress. If you are slow to add this responsibility, you risk underutilizing your employee and creating a scenario where they are not capable of taking more on.

These first few months are like a workout. At first, you've got to start with some stretches, and then you've got to push your body beyond its comfort zone to grow endurance and muscle. If you aren't pushing yourself, you won't gain strength and endurance.

In the 90s, I was hooked on a video game called SimCity. I spent hours on my PC trying to be the best mayor. It was the mayor's job to expand the city within the budget, deciding which buildings to build, where to put parks and recreation, and how to build out traffic flows and power grids, and you did all of it with the taxpayers' money.

At first, my cities constantly failed. People would rebel against me as soon as I had to raise taxes for capital funds for expansion. One day, as I was laying the foundation for a brand-new city, I had this master plan. I was going to start with high taxes and see what happened. I set the tax rate beyond what I actually needed for that moment, knowing that later, when I needed that money, I didn't have to raise taxes. It worked. I expanded further than I'd ever been able to expand before.

From this, I learned that if I set high expectations and eventually lower them, the people will rejoice. Funny enough, this actually works in business, too. When we set high expectations, we achieve higher results than when we set low expectations. When we need to raise expectations, we will always get more pushback than when we lower expectations. This is why some managers ask for 110%. It's the same concept as the BHAG, Big Hairy Audacious Goal. Pushing employees has a time and place, but like all things, it's fit for specific purposes and shouldn't be used all the time. If you're constantly forcing your team to go above and beyond with no end in sight, they won't have any reserve to weather storms. They also are in sustainability mode all the time and can't move into growth mode.

If you have ten people giving 110%, you've essentially added a headcount to your team. This is great until someone goes out on vacation or sick leave. If you have to replace someone who's learning at the 80% mark, you're going to have a difference between the 80 and 110%, or 30%. Where does that difference land? Usually on your other employees. You're going to burn them out in no time.

10 ppl at 110% = 1,100%
Divide the loss of productivity across the remaining resources
(30%/9 = 3.33%):
1 person at 80% + 9 ppl at 113.33% = 1,100%
Your team was already working at the breaking point,
and this added 3%, (only 3%!) could be the straw
that breaks the whole system.
More likely, one person is a superstar who is taking on
the extra work, which looks like this:
P1 = 80% (lost 30% from PTO)
P2 = 120% = dying (picked up 10% of the lost 30%)

P3 - P10 = 111% = feeling very strained (but no extra work done,
just 1% extra utilization drain from the "stress" of the work)
Dropped work - 20%
→ Total = 1108%

In this scenario, you're not getting more capacity. You're stressing out several of your employees, who are carrying the burden of the stress and are less productive because of it. You're burning out one employee who will either leave or make a critical mistake from being overburdened, and it's likely your superstar. This is a huge risk because it's the superstars who could decide this is not worth it and walk. That would create a catastrophic event for your team.

The solution is to staff right—not with 110% in mind, and not even with 100% in mind. Staff with 80% in mind for full capacity, knowing the other 20% is going to things like vacation, sick time, admin time, and special projects.

This doesn't mean that you don't work the team at each person's maximum efficiency level. It simply means you plan the BAU, or business as usual, for 80%, knowing that the other 20% will be taken with unknown factors.

Remember, to scale, you have to account for the sustainability of BAU and progression forward. To progress, you have to have some bandwidth to explore new concepts. To sustain, you have to have some bandwidth for "break-fixes."

Once you get the headcount, you need to run your operation, it's very important to keep the governance in mind as part of BAU operations.

Aha #48: Train up, even when it's harder.

To scale, you need to recognize the value of constant training.

Train up, even when it's harder for you to do so. If you have certain things you can teach others to do, you should teach them. This puts you in a much better position than being the only one who can do it. Too many new managers do it themselves because it's easier than training. But remember, easy choices lead to the hard road later on, and hard choices lead to easier ones later on.

Taking on something hard now for better results later comes from the Buddhist concept of suffering. We all suffer, and there's a path to easing that suffering, but that path is not always the most obvious one. Sometimes, Buddhists intentionally put themselves in situations of suffering for various reasons, mostly leading to the ultimate relief of suffering. To put it in more Western terms, delayed gratification pays exponentially in the long run.

I spend most of my time developing others, and sometimes, I develop them to leave my team. I've developed multiple people into being able to handle director-level roles, and then they've gone on to lead organizations outside of my remit. Here's the thing. I want my team filled with people who are smarter than I am. If they leave because I've given them the skills to do so, then, hopefully, they will do better for this world, and it will come back to me. But I never worry about that because I value my team. By limiting them, I limit myself.

Instead, I train them up and give them the skills to do whatever they want to do. If that's with me, I benefit. If it's not with me, the world still benefits, and therefore, I benefit. As Richard Branson, an influential businessman and founder of the Virgin Group, says, "Train people well enough so they can leave, treat them well enough so they don't want to."

What are some cues that you need to retrain a team rather than develop an individual?

When you see mistakes repeating themselves, it's an indicator that you need to train the broader team. If you see one person doing something wrong, retrain that individual. If you see two or more people doing it, the challenge is probably more widespread. Give the team a refresher course, or better yet, identify a trusted expert to train the team.

Aha #49: The higher up the management level, the more resources there are at your disposal.

Just as managers at all levels have the secret of leveraging others' learnings as their own, senior managers and leaders have the secret of leveraging resources in their downline as their own. I'm able to build systems that work for me, but sometimes, things don't go as expected. If everything stopped working at once, it would be beyond my capacity to support them all. Once the systems are set up, my job is to make sure the systems are reinforced so they don't break. I do this by developing others to lead the system.

If you're on the front line, you don't have that luxury. The only person to do the job is you. The job of a leader is to set the vision and put the systems in place to operate. As part of that, leaders have developed the right level of system reinforcement. Too little reinforcement and the system falls apart at catastrophic levels. Too much reinforcement and you have overage and waste. Too much reinforcement may even make the system too rigid, which will cause it to get outdated. As with all things, it's a balance.

Trust and Empathy

We've been using the analogy of building a house, where we have to get the foundation right before we build the frame. If the leader qualities are the foundation and the scalable system is the frame, then trust connects it all together. When you build trust, you're building a pathway between two systems, allowing the systems to work together.

Trust is what connects them and helps them work together. When trust is present, you're able to do things more quickly and without oversight.

When trust is broken, there is nothing more important than rebuilding it. This is why honesty is a leader quality, as are humility, graciousness, mercy, and empathy. They are all fundamental to building trust.

When empathy is involved in the trust dynamic, you have an especially powerful multiplier for scale because seeing things from another's perspective allows you to learn from their experiences without having to experience them yourself.

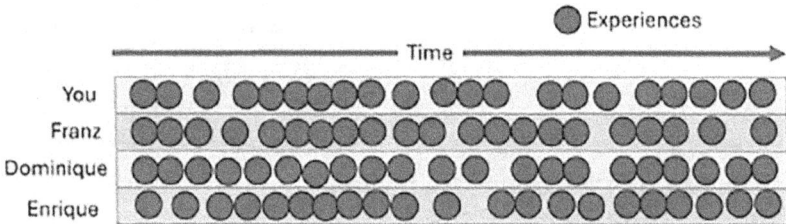

The image above depicts a certain number of experiences over a certain period. During that period, Franz, Dominique, and Enrique all have different experiences. If you have developed trust bonds with them, you can accept their experiences and take in the information that they gained from them without needing to have the experience yourself. You are now informed at a level that's four times what you could be on your own. You can make better decisions.

When you are surrounded by people you trust, not only will you make better decisions, but you will need to make fewer decisions because your trusted advisors will make them in accordance with your expectations and values.

When you can trust your employees to make decisions, you should empower them to make those decisions. Every. Time. While you were directing, you taught them the basic principles of what they need to make decisions. You reinforced it when you were coaching and mentoring. Now that they are experts, you can step back and focus on other areas.

Sometimes, employees don't think that they're ready to make those decisions on their own, even when we know that they're ready for it. To deal with this, let's look at the ideas of Jeff Bezos and Naval Ravikant.

Jeff Bezos has a rule about big and small decisions, where the big decisions are those that cannot be recovered from, whereas small decisions are ones from which you can come back if you choose the wrong path. He calls these decisions one-way and two-way doors. He encourages lower levels to make all the two-way-door decisions possible, and he keeps the one-way-door decisions at the highest levels. Bezos realized that the big decisions are like walking through one-way doors. These are decisions that you can't come back from. Once you walk through that door, you can't turn around, and the most senior executives should make these decisions.

Do you remember the section on time where we talked about the amount of time you should give to high- and low-impact decisions and that the highest-impact decisions should come from the resources with the highest judgment? That concept came from the well-known entrepreneur and AngelList founder Naval Ravikant, as described by Eric Jorgenson.

Now let's link the concepts of Naval and Bezos. If the decision is a two-way door, then the people who haven't yet refined their judgment should be empowered to make those decisions because the best way to learn is not by our successes but by our mistakes. But these are two-way doors; if they've made a mistake, they can always walk back. It goes both ways. They can quickly course-correct, and you're still on the right path in the end. Now, for full disclosure, I just connected this a couple of months ago as I was researching various elements for this book.

So, here's what I tell my team now. When the decision is a two-way door, they should consult with their peers but also feel empowered to make those decisions all day long. If the decision is a one-way door, they should consult with their peers to ensure that they have all their inputs, and if everyone agrees, they just need to keep me posted on what the decision was. If the peer group is not unanimous on the decision, then they should pull in me and/or their leader to make the decision.

By empowering the team to make these decisions, I'm showing

them that I trust them, and that is putting money back in the bank, which they can then—watch this now—invest and grow. I don't want them to sit on the money and end up with the same value that I gave them when I taught them the initial principle. Instead, I want them to grow their judgment so I can trust them with even bigger situations.

Those who can't be trusted with even little things will receive less, but those who can be trusted with much will receive even more.

> This is the moral of the New Testament story of the parable of the ten minas from Luke 19:11–27.

Stephen M. R. Covey (Stephen Covey's son) wrote the book on how trust generates speed in business: *The SPEED of Trust: The One Thing That Changes Everything*. In his book, he describes how trust is gained in waves that start with yourself and build outward with others. I'd like to expand on that a bit and say that the trust of others is gained from their credibility (what they have done) and your empathy (your ability to see things from their perspective). I'd also add that trust is earned from others through your credibility (what you've done) and humility (your honesty toward what you've done).

To trust others	Their credibility + Your empathy
To be trusted	Your credibility + Your humility

Your credibility is your currency for potential. If you're highly credible, you're trustworthy to make good decisions and execute well-planned strategies. Credibility is also a trust enabler. If you're credible, you're trusted. If you're not credible, you're not trusted. Think about all the people you trust the least. Now think about their credibility.

Aha #50: Be tireless in maintaining your credibility.

You see this in ancient wisdom all over the place—and when I see things repeated through history, I listen up.

As Aesop said, "A liar will not be believed even when he speaks the truth." Considering Aesop is believed to have lived around 620-564 BCE, and this concept still rings true today, it's worth our attention.

Regaining credibility takes too much time and energy, something that could have been avoided if one simply had not lost credibility to begin with.

Naval emphasizes the importance of judgment and credibility in building a successful career. He says, "To build a career, turn your ability into credibility." Credibility is the currency that adds up to people's value of your judgment. You build credibility through your actions. Your ability to make good decisions must be backed by a track record of success to be trusted by others.

Dispute resolution

Empathy is our trust in others expressed in our behavior. When you are empathetic, you can see things from the perspective of others and act upon that knowledge. When we trust another to have our best interest in mind, we're more likely to be able to put ourselves in their shoes and try to see the truth from their perspective. This takes humility (acknowledgment that our perspective may be limited) and courage (willingness to be vulnerable to another perspective). A connected leader uses empathy at scale to get to the underlying truths. This is an important skill to enable swift dispute resolution, which is a skill needed for a leader at any business of scale.

People tend to magnify their own world. And there will, of course, be times when worlds collide. A leader's job is to remove obstacles. If worlds colliding is not something the employees can solve for themselves, the leader plays the role of judge and jury. I find that when two employees disagree on a situation that has occurred or two parties don't agree on the same path forward, when I listen to each perspective empathetically, trying to really see where their truth might hold true for them, I can usually find a reality somewhere in the middle and help each get to a common ground from which they can move forward. This, too, requires trust. I trust that one person is not out to get the other.

Now allow me to elaborate on what I said earlier about trust. Trust is not the pathway between two systems. Networking is the pathway between systems. Trust is the power that flows through the network.

Networking

The old networking adage, "The sum of the parts is greater than the whole," reminds me of chemistry. In chemistry, atoms are the basic building blocks of all living and nonliving things. Atoms interact and connect.

When two or more atoms connect, they create a molecule. Sometimes, the same type of atoms connect, such as hydrogen atoms connecting in a hydrogen bond, and sometimes, atoms of different elements connect. For instance, two hydrogens and oxygen make H_2O. Now you have something quite different. You have water. Networking is like chemistry. You can do more and make up different things when you use your network.

Remember how we leverage our time, money, and resources to make systems work at scale? Wouldn't it be great if there were a silver bullet for this? Good news! There is—**networking**. We could not have a scalable solution for people without talking about the extreme leverage that's gained through networking.

Relationships bring the power to the entire system. Without rela-

162

tionships or others to support or share in the knowledge of work, we are limited to what we can do individually.

Networking allows you to not have to be the expert in everything.

Aha #18 shows up here again. Knowledge comes in two forms: what you already know and knowing where to find what you don't.

Who you know is possibly even more important than what you know. This is hard for many people to understand because they still feel the need to be the expert. They feel less valuable when they're not the go-to for everything. But knowing a lot of people and building a relationship in which you can leverage the knowledge or execution power of the people you know is even more valuable than having a know-it-all on the team. The network's value is exponentially greater. Networking is the path connecting the circuits.

You have an extremely powerful processing chip, but if you can't get your data to the right place, your knowledge is for naught. That's why trust is the power that flows through the network. The key here is not just knowing a lot of people but knowing a lot about those people. What do they do? What do they know? How can you help them, and how can they help you?

I said this was the only way to a scalable solution because you don't have to be the expert in everything. In fact, don't waste your time. You can only be an expert in a finite number of things, but you can know a number of people whose combined knowledge and expertise make you ten times or even a hundred times more valuable than you could be alone.

Someone once told me that networking felt gross. It took me a minute to gain this perspective because I've never thought of networking like that. But after listening intently to what this person was telling me, I discovered that she understood networking to be meeting a bunch of people whom you could use when the time was right. She thought of "use" as a one-way street. After talking with me, she realized that networking is not one-way; it's two-way. When you become interdependent on others, you're creating a system where they depend upon you and you on them. You're an asset to their network because you have the knowledge and leverage that you can then bring to the table for others.

Aha #51: Most people like to be helpful.

Allowing others to help and support you, especially if that support is something they can uniquely provide, can actually give them energy and confidence. I used to think that by asking for help, I was creating a burden, and I didn't want to be a burden on anyone. It took me a long time to realize that asking another person for help was being kind to them.

It's a gift because it allows them to shine if it's something they're strong in, and it allows them to grow if it's not their natural strength. But the key is to be genuine. You can't use your request for help as a crutch. You have to show that you've explored your options first, that you appreciate the gift they give, and that you'll use it. As I said, networking works if it's a two-way street. I fully expect to be able to help those who help me. Heck, I expect to be able to help those who do not help me now.

Helping each other allows energy to flow freely through systems. The flow of energy brings valuable things with it. When the flow is broken for any reason, both sides suffer. It's simple physics, going back to the conservation of energy. Energy can neither be created nor destroyed; it can only be converted from one form of energy to another.

The Leader Connection

Summary: In Chapter 8, we covered the beginner's mind and introduced the reader to the transformation tools of Six Sigma, Lean, Agile, and Scrum. We learned that leverage allows for scale and we discussed how to leverage a company's resources of time, money, and people. We talked about three dynamics of note: **judgment** and how you should shift decisions as a person gains judgment; my **theory of maximum efficiency**, where overloading workers creates a drain inversely proportionate to the overload; and finally, **trust**, which brings speed and breadth to the system. Everything in business is built on relationships. Relationships bring the power to the system, and networking is the path connecting the circuits. Remember this: relationships are the giant eraser that covers a multitude of missteps in a partnership, and trust is the giant enabler that allows you to go farther.

Chapter 9
The Journey to Growth

"You don't learn to walk by following the rules.
You learn by doing and falling over."
– Richard Branson

I tell new hires that they'll be confused for the first few weeks and then, one day, it'll click. At about the six-month mark, they're going to think they know what they're doing, and they're going to feel like they've finally got this in the bag. And right when they are feeling nice and comfy in their role, that's when they're going to come across something that knocks them on their butt and shatters them. When they pick up the pieces and put them back together, they're going to learn that they're stronger than before. This is the world of breakthroughs.

That analogy holds for administrators, professionals, and leaders. In fact, it holds true in almost any knowledge worker's role.

I've written this book about that journey. If you can't see it yet, let me help you with your perspective by giving you the roadmap.

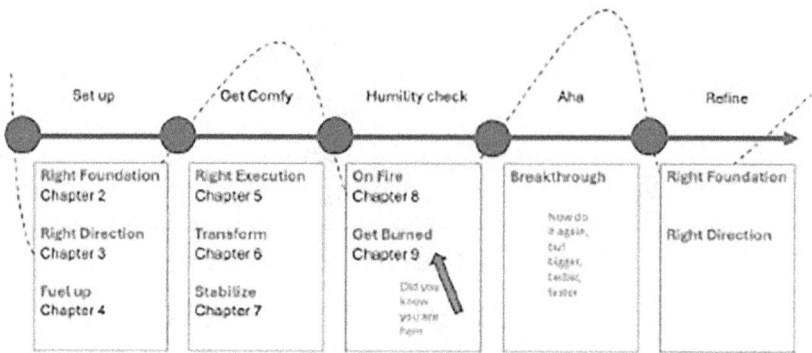

In Chapter 2, we discussed building the right foundation and the qualities needed to be a connected leader. Chapter 3 was about the right direction, how we need to begin with the end in mind, get pointed right, and, if we find ourselves off course, simply realign and repoint. Chapter 4 was about the ways to fuel the team. Chapter 5 was all about execution. By Chapters 6 and 7, you were ready to take the leap from explorer to sustainability. Chapter 8 was about how to use all that knowledge and create leverage to scale it. You were on fire.

But you know what Chapter 9 brings? If you're on fire, you might get burned, or more likely, you'll eventually burn out. But don't worry about going through the fire. If you set yourself up right in the prior chapters, you won't go through the fire. Instead, you will grow through the fire, and it's going to help you have your breakthrough.

I was in my mid-20s, and I'd been assigned my first management role. Not only that, but I was leading a team I knew very little about, sourcing or finding candidates for jobs. This was before LinkedIn, and I was responsible for the team that found out who worked at what companies and in what roles.

Then "they" gave me another team: advertising, an area I had no experience in. Here, I found myself calling newspapers, radio stations, and billboard companies to advertise job fairs across the country. But then, once again, "they" gave me another team. I wasn't equipped to manage so many people. Soon, I found myself with 35 direct reports with no formal coaching on leadership and managing, developing sourcing strategies, advertising plans, and recruitment scripts, hiring people, training them, or tracking everything. I had no clue what I was doing.

Fortunately, I had the foresight to find a mentor I could be really raw with. The person I found had a background in engineering and was a Six Sigma and Lean Sigma expert. She heard my story and immediately knew my problem. "You don't have enough tools in your toolkit," she said. Naive me thought: What tools? What toolkit? Nobody had given me a toolkit or tools to use. "They" had thrown me into the fire and expected me to figure it out. Then she explained to me that I was trying to build a house without the right tools and that if no one was going to give me the tools that I needed, it was my job to go searching in the garage and find them.

I did—and I have organized them and tucked them into this book so that you can find them a little more easily.

Another throwback to Aha #18, knowledge is of two kinds. If anyone knows Mrs. Kowalski, please give her this book. I'd like to thank her for taking the time to teach me something outside of our Spanish curriculum. I've spent the rest of my life trying to be Mrs. Kowalski for others.

Climb That Mountain!

What do you do when you climb a mountain? You prepare and get your tools ready, but essentially, you do it one step at a time. That's the key to execution. You take any problem or any challenge you have, break it down into the smallest achievable steps, and start hacking away. Stop worrying about how you're going to climb the whole mountain. Start with a plan on your very first step.

When I don't know what to do, I realize I don't have to know all the steps. All I need to know is the next best step, and that's what I do. After that, I take an inventory of where I'm positioned, along with all my options, and then I pick my next best step, and so on. I don't always get to my destination the fastest way possible, but I always end up getting there.

Did you know that the butterfly effect works on the micro but not on the macro? In chaos theory, the butterfly effect explains how small changes can lead to large changes at scale. This was evidenced by Edward Lorenz, who was working on weather prediction models. He dropped some of the extreme digits in the models and rounded them instead and came up with significantly different weather predictions. Lorenz was the first to publish his findings with the simile of a butterfly flapping its wings. He realized that small changes in the millionths of a single digit could mean enormous differences.

While this theoretically works in a vacuum at scale, at cosmos-level scale, as seen in quantum physics, unexpected results occur. Los Alamos scientists discovered that when you apply the butterfly effect at quantum levels across time, the disruptions do not spiral out of control as expected. Instead, string theory takes hold, and the stabilizers at scale counter the impact of the disruption. Over time and at extremely large scales, everything balances back out. If you are connecting with me, this is good news! Take the risks because everything balances out over time. It's going to be okay because it has always been okay.

Break-Fixes at Scale

Eventually, things will break. Because you've climbed the mountain, you've scaled your team. When things break now, they have the potential to cause massive disruption in your organization. If this happens, the first thing you need to do is stop the bleeding. Put on the metaphorical tourniquet and cut off the blood supply to the bleeding area. Once the bleeding has stopped, check in with everyone to determine what kind of damage control is needed.

Finally, you need to identify why things broke in the first place and ensure it never happens again. That's where root-cause analysis comes in, or RCA. The point of root-cause analysis is not just to identify the source of the problem but to correct it.

My favorite RCA is the "five whys" method, where you ask, "Why did the problem occur?" After you answer, you ask why that occurred and then keep going until you get to five whys.

For instance,

Problem: the report didn't get completed on time

Why 1: Why was the report late? Answer: Because Susan didn't finish it in time.

Why 2: Why didn't Susan finish it on time? Answer: Because she didn't have all her information in time.

Why 3: Why didn't Susan have all her information in time? Answer: Because Jill only gave her part of the information, and Susan had to chase her.

Why 4: Why did Jill only have part of the information? Answer: Because there was a filter on the source data.

Why 5: Why was there a filter on the source data? Answer: Because multiple people go in and can set the filters to their view.

There it is—the filters don't reset after every use, which is causing data integrity issues. Fix the process.

You usually uncover the root cause around the fourth or fifth why. At the top layers, you're uncovering symptoms. When you try to fix the symptoms, you haven't gotten to the source of the problem, and the problem will reoccur. At the bottom layers, you're uncovering the root cause.

During your RCA, you may find that your process was solid but wasn't executed as it was intended.

Remember when we talked about the Israelites coming out of Egypt and how, when things got tough, some of them went back to their old ways? We learned that our natural habits will come out when things get tough. If the process was designed well but the team did not execute it correctly, that's because their natural habits led them down a different path.

When this happens, your job is to find out what it was that enticed them to the other path and then remove the obstacles blocking the right path. Was the other path easier? Then you can make it harder. Was the right path too difficult to understand or execute? Did your employee need more education, guidance, or enforcement? You get to put on your sleuth hat or tap your mini-COO on the shoulder to uncover what needs to be addressed for flawless execution.

Aha #52: Remove your obstacles.

Hopefully, this is self-explanatory. Several times, I've mentioned that one of the main jobs of a leader is to identify and remove obstacles.

It took me forever to realize I was my hardest obstacle to remove. Now, what does that mean? All my external obstacles made sense. Therefore, they were easier to identify and correct. But my internal obstacles were less apparent to me. I learned to see more of them when I was working with others and started holding up a mirror to myself to see if the mirror test panned out.

As I was working with other people, I would get frustrated when I told them to do something, and they couldn't do it. I would then show them how to do it, and they still sometimes didn't do it. These people always had a great excuse for why they couldn't do the job, and it sounded really plausible when they said it. If it hadn't been for the fact that I could do the job I was asking for, I would have believed their excuse. But I knew I could do it, so I knew they could, too. They couldn't see that their thinking was getting in their own way of execution. This is where the mirror test worked.

If this sounds familiar, it should. It's connected to Aha #1: Managers learn from their employees. The mirror test allows us to see in ourselves what we learn from others.

I assumed that if my employees were periodically blinded by their own way of thinking, that must mean that I, too, must be periodically blinded by my own way of thinking. As it turns out, I am! Sometimes, I get so mired in the details and connections that I forget to step back and take an inventory of my prospective options. However, because I am aware of this, I am more likely to catch myself faster and course-correct.

This is an example of how I use the Pointed Right Model in Chapter 3.

Aha #53: When faced with many obstacles, first remove the ones that prevent the most people from achieving success.

Have you ever been in a situation where everything is going wrong all at once? It's like the universe knows when to hit you from every direction. There's a reason we named this Murphy's law. It's universal. I had the honor of being mentored by Darren Findley, the president of Recruitment Solutions at Engage2Excel. I asked him what I should do in a particularly tough situation. He said, "Shanda, when the whole forest is on fire, which tree do you put out first?"

I answered the most intelligent way I knew how at the time: "I don't know, Darren, that's why I'm asking you."

And then he said, "The one next to the gas station, of course."

Aha! Identify which fire is about to spread and create more havoc, and then put out that fire first. Another way of looking at this is to identify which challenge has the potential to negatively impact the most number of people and address it first.

Connected leader moment: Remember when we talked about the "one thing" philosophy and how doing that one thing removes a lot of other, smaller things? The principle works with both goals and in obstacle reduction (firefighting) scenarios. Can you identify one fire that, if it went out, would save you from having to put out more fires in the future? That's the fire you put out first.

Aha #54: Interruption of flow costs time, money, and people.

As business scales, overhead costs increase at disproportionate rates. Think about this for a moment. One would expect overhead to decrease with scale. In some cases, it does, but a series of waste is also created with diversification because of the interruption of flow from one unit to another. Flow state is where things are flowing naturally, and it's the most optimized state.

Throwback to Gay Hendrick's The Genius Zone *discussed in Chapter 4.*

Flow state occurs both at an individual and an organization level. Interrupters of the flow state at an individual level would be things like distractions, meetings, and switching tasks.

I'm a proponent of flexible working opportunities. If a person is in their best flow in the office and around others, where gaining insight from others is easier in person, then it's on the leader to ensure they have a space that they can go to where others are around. If a person is in their best flow at home, where they don't have office interruptions or a commute, then they should be able to work from home. As with all things, it's a balance. If half of the office worked remotely, that's half as many resources available in person for those who want the in-person experience. Some people thrive with people around them, and that's how they gain their energy. This, too, can be a sort of flow state. Some people get drained by being around people, and managers who force them to come in are reducing the flow of the organization.

Interruptions to flow state at an organizational level would be things like handoffs between roles and busy work that's not optimized. As we saw in Chapter 6, as a company grows in scale, it needs more specialized roles. This specialization causes more handoff points between resources and those interrupt flow.

You need to be able to work outside of the lines when you're in a nomadic state of exploration. But when you're in a sustainable state, the settlers, you need to have clear delineation. Over time, those nomads will create a gray area in the delineation, and then that gray area gets left for others. Your job is to ensure this is periodically cleaned up.

Aha #55: Sometimes, you have to enjoy the interruption!

A connected leader looks for the areas of unnecessary flow state interruption at both an individual and organizational level and reduces them.

By the way, this is what Six Sigma and Lean Sigma do for processes.

When cutting out distractions, however, it's important to recognize which distractions are truly momentum killers, thus reducing kinetic energy and which are actually energy credits that are building up potential energy for the future. Sometimes, the interruptions are the breaks needed to get a new perspective.

Meetings are a great example of this. We already know that meeting for meeting's sake can often be a distraction. Your job as a leader is to ensure that every meeting adds value for your team. Every. Meeting. If the content is not adding value, cancel the meeting.

Breakroom chats are another example of this. Obviously, we don't want the team ignoring their responsibilities, but not only can break-room banter re-engage people, but it can also bring people together who would not normally have collaborated. It can foster great ideas and drive company culture in ways that formal training never could.

Give them a break. To ensure it's not interrupting the flow state, let them pick when and how long. As long as you have a clear set of objectives and you've set your expectations in advance, giving your team the freedom to navigate these things will help them be more productive. If you're finding a few bad eggs who are taking advantage of their freedom, you will fare better if you manage the root cause (misplaced prioritization), not the symptom (excessive breaks). You're likely seeing reduced productivity due to their lack of prioritization, and that's something you can manage more easily. When you see the output dip, you go back to the person and assess their performance against their objectives.

Aha #56: Automation provides maximum efficiency flow for time, money, *and* people.

Adding technology and automating as much as possible is a way to reduce your resources, create additional time, and reduce costs. Neil Pasricha, a podcaster, author, and entrepreneur, says that he has a secret to never being busy again. In *The Happiness Equation*, he says that we're making three hundred decisions a day and are overloaded with them. He proposes that you find a way to automate as many decisions as possible. By automation, he means programming it into your routine to remove the choice.

Here's how it shows up for me. I fill the time in my days with work and family. Eating home-cooked meals at the kitchen table with my family is important to me, and I like having variety in my food, but I dislike the process of carving out time to decide days in advance what I'm going to eat so I can ensure I have the right groceries, etc. Instead, I choose boxed meal kit deliveries to show up at my door so I don't have to decide what meal to make and don't have to buy all the ingredients. I just open up a box of fresh food and make the meal inside.

My grocery list then looks like a list of rinse-and-repeat items that I buy weekly. It's the kind of automation that Pasricha is talking about. I take the decisions out of my day that I don't care about or don't want, and I weave in the decisions that are important to me.

We've talked about giving people the freedom to choose how to get to an outcome, but some things need to be done a certain way. The path is part of the outcome and cannot be separated from it. For these things, I ensure there are clear expectations and written instructions that can be followed. Organization is a kind of automation. It's why process maps and SOPs bring efficiency to the workplace. This is Pasricha's kind of automation.

Aha #57: "Saying yes to something means saying no to something else."

Tim Ferriss, author, podcaster, and investor, is best known for books like *The 4-Hour Workweek* and *Tools of Titans*. I regularly listen to his podcast, which is rich with ideas and habits from highly successful people. In several of his podcasts, Tim pointed out that when you agree to do something, there's always something else you cannot do with that time. Tim uses the example that if he agrees to review a book, it means he has to read the book, or if he's agreed to give the speech, it means time is taken away from what he really wants to be doing. While I first connected the importance of this idea from Tim, I'm not sure where the saying originated. Some attribute it to Ryan Holiday, a popular author and blogger. Considering that through his podcast, Tim introduced me to a lot of Holiday's books, it would make sense that Tim could have been referencing one of Holiday's concepts. Either way, it's a great Aha.

Connected leader moment: This is closely connected to filling your time with the big block items first, the things that will give you the biggest impact on the time spent. Impact can be measured in tangible results, such as revenue, but it can also be measured in potential results, such as quality of life, as in Tim's example. This is the same as energy credits, whether it be kinetic or potential energy. When you say yes to something, you're agreeing to spend a certain amount of energy on it.

"Do whatever gives you the most energy. Because energy is that currency that drives almost everything else."
—Tim Ferriss, SXSW, 2023

Connecting this back to what we said in Chapter 7 about how we should leverage money, replace the question I asked about money with "energy." Ask yourself: by spending that energy, are you multiplying your energy or draining it?

The more you say yes to something, the more people are going to let you do it. It's the path of least resistance, which is a physical phenomenon describing how most matter flows along the path that resists its movement the least, but it describes human behavior, too.

Connect this: In Taoism, the Wei Wu Wei, or action through non-action, suggests that things will flow naturally. Again, it's the path of least resistance. Those who say yes will get more of the same, and those who say no will, too.

Do you find yourself saying yes because, if not you, then who? This is where you need a shadow buddy.

Aha #58: Be the squeaky wheel.

The squeakiest wheel gets oiled first. We all know that person who is annoying, that pushy leader who, if we don't do what they really want, will drive us nuts until we do it. What should you learn from them? If you want something done, be the squeaky wheel. Don't give up on voicing your needs or concerns. Others will attend to you to get you to stop squeaking.

This comes from the parable of the persistent widow and the judge from Luke 18:1–8.

Aha #59: Overuse is just as bad as underuse.

My grandmother used to say, "Too much of anything, no matter how good it is, is good for nothing." I feel it necessary to point out that, sometimes, overuse of good qualities can be bad. For instance, empathy is very important, but when not selective, empathy can turn into choosing sides and creating drama and friction within a team.

Everyone has that natural quality that makes them great, but, when overused, is a limiter. For me, it's details. I'm extremely detail-oriented, which is fantastic for my credibility and makes people think I'm smart, but people also get lost in the details and can zone out if I'm not using them at the right time. And let's not forget how details can trap me into a perspective. I can find myself diving so deep into the details that I forget to see the forest for the trees.

This is connected to Aha #34: what got you here won't get you there.

Aha #60: Do not enable bad behavior.

Here is a spattering of some of the most common bad behaviors that I see the manager allow their employees to continue to do for far too long. We've already addressed solutions for several of these elsewhere, but here's a reference guide.

Behavior	Why it's a problem	What to do
Short-sighted	Short-term gain will cause long-term pain	Perspective, zoom out
Too nice	Unwilling to have difficult conversations.	Having difficult conversations is nice
Not organized	Short-term gain will cause long-term pain.	Organization
Too proactive	Missteps are made as the resource does not see the big picture yet.	Perspective, zoom out
Controlling	People think their way is the only way. They limit the possibility of a better way or even a better way for a different person.	Trust and Empathy
Forgetting the why	The why generates intrinsic motivation.	Share the why
Forgetting the how	The how removes obstacles to doing. It enables execution.	Show the how
Zooms too far in	The bigger picture gets lost. This could create issues with identifying the right priorities.	Perspective, zoom out
Doesn't zoom in far enough/not detail-oriented	Causes mistakes and incorrect assumptions	Perspective, zoom in
Fake	Breaks trust	Trust
Creates fractions	Breaks trust. Builds an us-versus-them environment.	Make "them" look good

Behavior	Why it's a problem	What to do
Dehumanizes	Breaks trust and demotivates the team.	Empathy
Not changing fast enough	You're losing momentum, and you're going to be left in the dust. This also happens when the job changes and the old resource was a fit for the old job but not the new one.	Momentum
Not changing for the situation	You're not meeting your employees where they are. This will frustrate the employees and stagnate their growth.	Style Awareness Guide
Fear-based leading	Momentum is lost, energy is drained, and short-term gain causes long-term pain.	Trust and Empathy
Poor communication	There are many reasons this is bad. Here are a few: Breaks trust. Demotivates team. Causes mistakes. Leads to incorrect assumptions.	360-degree communication

Burnout

Aha #61: When things get tough, our natural state comes out.

During the section on "break-fixes" at scale, I mentioned that when things get tough, our natural state comes out. Burnout is caused when your natural state is not in line with your ideal state. If you were in your ideal state, you would have all the resources to do whatever you needed to do naturally. You would have an abundant amount of energy and not burn out in your lifetime. But since your natural state is sure to fall short, you then have to work in overdrive to overcome your short callings. This leads to burnout.

Not sold? Consider this. If you're not accepting that the gap is within you, you're looking for external sources to place the blame on for your shortcomings, or you don't believe that you have any shortcomings. If it's the latter, go check your humility. If it's the former, wherever your blame is if you had everything you needed within you to overcome any external adversity you face, could you not use your resources to get you out of the pickle?

There's a third path here: enjoy the pickle. You may not have all the resources you need. Fighting it is exhausting. If you relax in it, you may not advance as quickly, but you'll save yourself a lot of energy. I know this to be true, though I personally struggle with relaxing into the pickle. I'm getting better with time. Some leaders of very large teams, larger than mine in most cases, seem to naturally be able to relax in the pickle. I'm in awe of them.

My natural state falls brutally shy of a good leader. I was fortunate enough to be put through the wringer and stretched to the max, but that wringer wasn't strong enough to make me who I am today. I had to do a lot of networking, listening, and reading to complement my experiences with others' experiences.

Look back at the 11 qualities I mentioned in Chapter 2. I selected 11 for the specific reason of supporting the behaviors that I want those qualities to bring out: the behavior of gaining perspective, the behavior of building strong connections, and the behavior of application, specifically of applying principles learned from small-scale situations to large-scale solutions.

However, many leadership development programs and job profiles have even more qualities and competencies, up to 20 or more. Does everyone have all 20 or even 11? No. At best, we are really good at two or three of these. Even if we want to be good at all of them, two or three are default strengths that we're good at, even when things get tough.

Brené Brown has found the same to be true of leadership values. In Simon Sinek's A Bit of Optimism *Podcast, "Thinking about Thinking with Brené Brown and Adam Grant, part 2," she says that there are roughly 20 leadership values available. Everyone thinks they encompass all 20, but really, only two guide them through all situations. The others may show up here and there, but they're not consistent.*

There are qualities you are good at. These are the qualities you need to leverage—they are your natural strengths, so use them to your advantage. There are qualities you are improving in; keep that up. There are also qualities that you are not good at. These are the ones you need to learn. If it's too tough to learn them right now, surround yourself with a mini-C-suite complement of people who bring those qualities to the table.

None of us is perfect. That's a beautiful concept. It's not about our flaws; it's about our differences. If we were all perfect, we'd be cookie-cutter images of each other. Because we're not perfect, we need each other, and we need the fire to test us and make us stronger.

I hope you've learned a few tools for your toolkit as you journey through my leadership development story. And I can't wait to hear about those tools you picked up that someone else or another experience gave you. I'm not exhausted. I'm energized.

Aha #62: You will get through this. You always do.

Let me be crystal clear: walking through the fire is painful. I've been burned out many times. Each fire has brought me extreme stress and pain. But today, if I'm traveling through a fire I've been through before, it doesn't seem as hot or painful. That's because I've been adding to my toolkit along the way, and I guess I picked up some of those cooling blankets, i.e., the knowledge that I will get through this. I always do.

Some things that were not natural to me at the beginning, I have practiced so much that muscle memory has set in, and they're more natural to me now. There are some fires that I know I cannot manage again, so when I encounter them, I put up the safety gear to ensure that I don't get anywhere near them. This is called setting boundaries. As a human who is kind to yourself, find yours. As a leader of others, respect theirs. Bonus points to those leaders who can see when someone needs to get permission to create and maintain their boundaries and help those employees do it.

Unfortunately, some people use "boundaries" as an excuse for laziness. I liken it to cheating. If you understand and respect the principle of boundaries, it will do you well, but if you abuse it, you harm the rest of us. To those people, I ask, are you taking the hard way for the easy life or the easy way, which leads to the hard life?

If you're overworked, you'll continue to be overworked until you break the cycle. It's the law of attraction. When you're overworked, work finds you. Before I had all my tools, including the tool of appropriate boundaries, I worked around the clock. As a global leader, I took calls with India at 2 a.m., took a nap, led calls with the UK at 6 a.m., took calls with the US at 7 a.m., and worked straight until Pacific started logging off. I'd take a break to try and have a "healthy" dinner with my family, and then APAC would come around, and I'd be back on calls at 9 or 10 p.m., nap, India at 3 a.m., and then rinse and repeat.

It was my job to "fix" things, or so I thought. I was the "buck stops here" hero. People couldn't do it without me. But I was killing myself slowly. My body knew, but I wasn't listening. The problem with being the hero is that everyone relies on you to come in and take care of things, and then they don't do it themselves. I was like a helicopter parent. Recent studies show that while well intended, the fastest way to kill a child's confidence is to do things for them instead of letting them figure it out on their own. That's what I was doing to my team. I thought I was helping, but I was enabling bad behavior.

My personal boundaries were completely shot, too. I saw boundaries as a thing that only weak people used. Didn't I just get through saying the fire strengthens us? No pain, no gain, right? Sort of. Remember that law of max efficiency? Too many activities lead to lower output levels. This is when adding more fuel to the fire works against you. You're not only no longer making yourself stronger, but you're actually making yourself and your team weaker.

When I finally stepped away and gave myself the grace and space of 24 hours to break the cycle, I saw it:

Aha #63: Sometimes, 24 hours of perspective is all it takes.

Breakthrough

The best way to avoid burnout is to put systems in place to prevent you from getting there in the first place. The biggest lesson I've learned is to set up parameters to see the triggers that cause burnout and take action to move the needle. The chapters that lead up to here explain the systems and tools I use to

- Identify priorities.
- Remove the clutter.
- Build strong human connections through trust networks.
- Enable a culture of execution.
- Check-in on perspective and reset as needed.

It comes back to the qualities of perspective, connection, and application. We are back to our foundation, where we began.

Now do it again, but bigger, better, and faster.

Right Foundation

Right...

Of course we're doing it again. It's the law of polarity, which causes perpetual motion: the pendulum swings, and all things cycle. If you don't like the phase of the cycle you're in, wait a minute, and the phase you like better will come back. But it's pointless to fight the phase you're in now. Recognize it and support it so that it passes quickly. The fastest way past the storm is through it, head-on.

You're moving from seeing only a pixel, which is where we started, to seeing the whole picture, where you are a pixel. And there are hundreds of other pixels working together beautifully in one picture.

Summary: In Chapter 9, we talked about firefighting techniques at scale. Obviously, the best defense is a good offense, and it's important to put yourself in a situation to mitigate fires before they arise. Nonetheless, fires will occur, and they are devastating at scale. I gave you a handful of ideas on how to keep ahead of them. Perhaps one of my favorite learnings: we discussed saying "yes" to something really means we are saying "no" to something else. The necessity of that realization calls us to check our yeses, and it frees us to accept them for the nos that they really are.

Chapter 10
Back to the Basics

"Every morning, we are born again.
What we do today is what matters most."
– Buddha

When I'd been in management for a couple of years, and the business was booming, my boss came into my office and said, "I need you to get everyone back to the basics. Have your team pick up the phones and start cold calling leads."

At that time, I thought he was naive. Didn't he know that candidates would readily apply if he would just post the job on this new invention called a job board? In fact, there was a great one called Monster.com that was just getting started and that everyone was flocking to. There was also this other really cool search engine that had recently launched, called Google, where you could find candidate resumes. We didn't call it the digital age yet, but I knew we were moving into a new way of doing things. And here my boss was, stuck in his ancient ways.

Oh, how wrong I was.

Of course, there was a new way of doing things. And that way would eventually take off, but that didn't mean it was time to forget the things that worked. The digital age was going to create opportunities that had never existed at scale before, but it was going to create obstacles that had never existed at scale before, too. Chief among them is human connection. My boss had been supremely right that we needed to be on guard against removing the human connection.

Aha #64: Get back to the basics.

I live in Texas, where we have a saying: "It's not if you need foundation repair; it's when you'll need foundation repair." The climate here will eventually destroy your foundation. The climate in Texas may speed up foundational issues, but going back to the second law of thermodynamics, that entropy always increases, how fast this happens depends on external factors and how much reinforcement you put in along the way.

Take account of where you are and where you're going. Pull out the pointed right model periodically. Clean up your distractions. Start over with fresh eyes. Where are you now in relation to your foundation? Have you relied on interpretation upon interpretation, or have you gone back to the source and read it for yourself?

I call this getting back to the basics. Buddhists call it the beginner's mind. Whatever you call it, having a strong foundation will put you in a good position to be pointed right.

Recipe for success:

- Make yourself a strong foundation.
- Begin with the end in mind.
- Align your direction.
- Go and grow.
- Get back to the basics and refine your methods.
- Repeat.

Did you know that a word often used in the Hebrew Bible for "repent" is "SHV," which means to start over, return, or come back to something? It's an Aha on another scale. It's not about beating yourself up. It's about seeing your foundation and what it's meant to be and returning to it.

I like to tell my children that it's not enough to say they're sorry. They have to mean it. To me, sorry means that, if given the chance to do it over again, you wouldn't have done it the way you did it. That's what repenting means: turning back to the way things should be. Over time, different things cause us to lose perspective in business. This is where taking the moment to reset can be so powerful.

We start where we began, but we do it with a new lens. In his famous 2005 Stanford Commencement Address, Steve Jobs said, "Getting fired from Apple was the best thing that could have ever happened to me. The heaviness of being successful was replaced by the lightness of being a beginner again. It freed me to enter one of the most creative periods in my life."

When Jobs was fired from Apple, he created NeXT Computers, which Apple eventually bought, and they brought him back in. He took what he had learned in his venture with NeXT and did even greater things with Apple his second time around. Wouldn't it be great to have this perspective and opportunity without getting fired?

Aha #65: Reinvent yourself.

You have to step away and give yourself perspective. This means changing things up, taking a sabbatical, doing something different, acquiring new businesses, and putting someone else in charge for a while. You have two options: reinvent yourself or die. It's as simple as that.

The second law of thermodynamics and the law of entropy: To stay warm, you have to stay active.

The way to make the best choice and have the greatest judgment is to have the most perspective. Through perspective, you can better define the problem and your options. Getting back to the basics gives us perspective. It allows us to step outside the details of the day-to-day and take account of where we are. It gives us the opportunity to see things with fresh eyes.

Have you ever felt like you were just going around in circles? When you zoom out, you're not going in circles; you're climbing a spiral staircase upwards.

This is not my idea. I heard it somewhere and cannot recall where it came from, but I am hoping the concept is universal enough that we can all share in the wisdom.

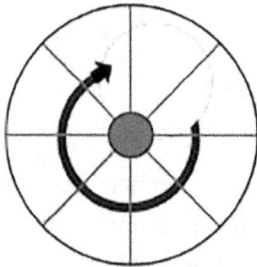

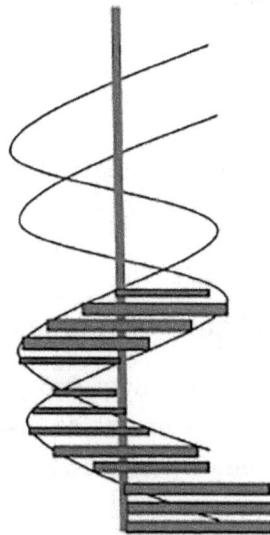

Everything is cyclical and diabolical. Expect this and embrace it. If you have enough inputs, similar to historical events and the levers that impact the change, eventually, not only can you predict what's yet to come, but you can influence it. This is what great investors do, and it's what data scientists do for predictive analysis.

Aha #66: You have an integral part of the puzzle.

As I said in Chapter I, you are the product of the people you meet, the books you've read, and the experiences you have. Other people can meet the same people you meet and read the same books you have read. Your experiences are uniquely yours. The connections you draw from those people, books, and experiences are yours to pass on to your team. I challenge you to use those connections to reinforce your team structure as it grows.

Your toolkit has to be filled with various tools, and you get to decide which one to use at which time. You can build a house using a hammer. You can even use that same hammer to crush a house, but you cannot use the hammer to paddle a boat. You need to recognize which tools will work in which situations because, if I know anything for sure, it's that things change, and as situations change, the tools you use may need to change, too. I've shared my journey with you and a myriad of Ahas along the way. I have no doubt that you already realize several of them, but I hope a few have resonated with you and you've picked them up along the way.

Returning to our qualities of a leader, I began with the end in mind on perspective, connection, and application, and I will begin again tomorrow. I'll take what I've learned on my journey, and I'll pack only those tools that serve me well, for the journey is long, and I want to travel light. So, it's your choice. Newton's first law states that an object at rest stays at rest, and an object in motion stays in motion. Do or don't, but whatever you choose, know that choice is always yours, and you're going to be asked to choose every day.

Exercise 10: Your Ahas

In the space that follows, add any of your Ahas that you've gained in your journey. We're adding the pieces to the puzzle or passing on the baton. It would be an honor if you'd add your fingerprints and pass it on.

Summary: The finish line is a man-made boundary that marks an opportunity – not to end the race, but to reflect on your growth through the journey and to begin the next segment stronger than before.

NOTES

NOTES

NOTES

Conclusion

I started this book with a great promise: I was going to take you on a journey with me through connections, and we'd pick up some tools along the way.

What fundamental truths do we see that withstand the test of time? Have I taken you there? Have we explored the laws of nature and physics? Have we talked about kinetic energy and potential energy, Newton's law of motion, Einstein's theories of relativity, the laws of thermodynamics, and the laws of conservation?

Have we talked about ancient teachings and principles found in Christianity, Judaism, Buddhism, Islam, and Taoism? Did we meet some ancient empire builders? Did we do a little math, history, and storytelling along the way? Have we explored these principles and how they show up with some of the more recent leaders and investors? Did you learn about some of the differences between small and large teams and the constant transformative push and pull between growth-oriented teams and stabilizers?

As I said in the beginning, the journey to growth is a challenging one. There's no secret or silver bullet. There's only a choice. When you choose to get your foundation right and get pointed right, when you choose to constantly execute well and reassess and repoint, you will end up where you need to go. I shared with you two rules for growth in Chapter 6: do what sells, and if it doesn't sell, don't do it.

Here are my two rules for sustaining scale:

1. When you grow outside the box, build a new box.
2. When you build a new box, cut a window and a door.

Build the box with governance, yes, but allow for flexibility in the design. Change is inevitable. Even as I am writing this journey about what it takes to grow and scale your teams, I am cognizant that many companies are in scale-back mode and not growth mode. This, too, is good. It allows us the space and opportunity to assess our metaphorical house and determine what improvements need to be made. This is a great time to think about setting ourselves up for success in the future.

As I've said many times, when you have the space available, fill it with the big block items—and your big blocks right now are things that will give you fuel for your potential energy:

1. Learn. You're rocking this one. This book was a learning journey.
2. Increase your revenue or decrease your costs. A lot of the tools in this book are designed to help you operationally in exactly these areas.
3. Gain market share. I didn't talk about how to expand your market share and all the skills it takes to fill your sales and marketing pipeline and funnel. These are areas others are more amply qualified to speak to. But don't forget this very important block as you are working towards scaling your business.
4. Create sustainable solutions. You have many new tools in your toolkit now to create sustainable teams.

Conclusion

Ending where we began, thank you for taking this journey with me. Thank you for taking in these lessons I've picked up along the way. Now that you have a better perspective, stronger connection, and know the power of application, I hope you have put a few more tools in your toolkit for your journey ahead.

See good. Be good. Do good. That's all you have to do. As you progress on your own journey, do me a favor and pick up a few of your own Ahas along the way and share them with your team. One day, they will be stronger because of your wisdom, and on another day, they will share their Ahas with future generations.

> *Bonus Material:* *For a consolidated list of all the Ahas, check out www.MintROI.com.*

It wasn't until I was editing this work that I realized there are some autobiographical undertones. I was not just writing about the typical manager-to-leader growth journey; it was my journey, too. You probably saw this coming way before I did.

I don't go around talking to my team about scientific theory and ancient teachings. I tease out the connections and themes for the end result, not for their history. This is a learning book. I am constantly learning. Future me may look back and have new lessons that change my perspective. I hope she does!

I gave significant effort to the research that went into this book and a lot of attention went to tracking down original sources. If I have misquoted or misattributed anyone, please don't hesitate to let me know at www.MintROI.com.

So many people contributed to this book. To everyone I have met, everyone who wrote books I've read, and everyone who contributed to experiences I have had, thank you. Yes, even you, the reader, whom I have not yet met, might have contributed. Most of all, thank you for giving me the gift of your time. I hope you have learned a few tools that will help you in your journey.

Conclusion

To Mrs. Kowalski and all the teachers who taught more than books ever could. THANK YOU.

To my children, Nathan and Zoe, and my husband, Mark, you guys are my guiding stars. When I get lost, you're always there to brighten my day or ground me in reality. Without your grace and support, I could not have shared these lessons with others.

I learn from each of you. I hope I have honored your gifts.

THANK YOU FOR READING MY BOOK!

DOWNLOAD YOUR FREE GIFTS

Just to say thanks for buying and reading my book, I would

like to give you a few free bonus gifts, no strings attached!

To Download Now, Visit:

I appreciate your interest in my book and value your feedback as it helps me improve future versions. I would appreciate it if you could leave your invaluable review on Amazon.com with your feedback.
Thank you!

References

1. "5-Whys Guide & Template." *Michigan.gov*, https://www.michigan.gov/-/
   media/Project/Websites/mde/2020/04/02/5_Whys_Worksheet.pdf?rev=
   1a4a151a2fbf4e56a0f88dd1ad43452f.
2. Adobe Communications Team. "BHAG (Big Hairy Audacious Goal)."
   Adobe Experience Cloud Blog, 18 Mar. 2022, https://business.adobe.com/
   blog/basics/bhag.
3. Alessandra, Tony, and Michael J. O'Connor. *The Platinum Rule*. Hachette
   UK, 2008.
4. "Alexander the Great." Encyclopædia Britannica, https://www.britanni-
   ca.com/biography/Alexander-the-Great.
5. Allen, David. *Getting Things Done*. Penguin, 2015.
6. "A Traditional Story of Tom Watson Forgiving a Sales Mistake."
   Discerning Readers, https://www.discerningreaders.com/watson-sr-we-
   forgive-thoughtful-mistakes.html.
7. Bezos, Jeffrey P. "Amazon Shareholder Letter, 1997." Amazon, https://s2.
   q4cdn.com/299287126/files/doc_financials/annual/
   Shareholderletter97.pdf
8. Bezos, Jeffrey P. "Amazon Shareholder Letter, 2016." Amazon, https://s2.
   q4cdn.com/299287126/files/doc_financials/annual/2016-Letter-to-
   Shareholders.pdf
9. "Bill Gates: Software Icon, Philanthropist." The Henry Ford,
   https://www.thehenryford.org/explore/stories-of-innovation/vi-
   sionaries/bill-gates/.
10. Blanchard, Ken, et al. *The One Minute Manager Anniversary Ed*. Harper
    Collins, 1982.
11. Bossidy, Larry, et al. *Execution: The Discipline of Getting Things Done*.
    Crown Currency, 2009.
12. Boswell, James. *Boswell's Life of Johnson*. 1901.
13. Caramela, Sammi. "10 Characteristics of a Successful Business." U.S.
    Chamber of Commerce, 23 July 2024, https://www.uschamber.-
    com/co/start/strategy/successful-businesses-common-characteristics.
14. Carroll, Sean. *Quanta and Fields*. Penguin, 2024.
15. Collins, Jim, and Jerry I. Porras. *Built to Last*. Harper Collins, 2011.
16. Covey, Stephen M. R. *The 7 Habits of Highly Effective People*. Simon and
    Schuster, 2004.

References

17. Covey, Stephen M. R. *The Speed of Trust*. Simon and Schuster, 2008.
18. Everett, Julee. "Scrum and Six Sigma: Can They Co-Exist?" LinkedIn, 26 Mar. 2018, https://www.linkedin.com/pulse/scrum-six-sigma-can-co-exist-julee-bellomo-everett#:~:text=There%20are%20many%20best%20practices,the%20pursuit%20of%20continuous%20improvement.
19. Ferriss, Tim (Host). (2024). The Tim Ferris Show [Audio podcast]. Tim Ferriss Productions. https:tim.blog/podcast/
20. "General Relativity." Wikipedia, https://en.wikipedia.org/wiki/General_relativity.
21. "Genghis Khan: Descendants, Empire & Facts." History, https://www.history.com/topics/asian-history/genghis-khan.
22. "Getting Things Done®: David Allen's GTD® Methodology." Getting Things Done®, https://www.facebook.com/gettingthingsdone/, https://gettingthingsdone.com/.
23. Goleman, Daniel. *Working With Emotional Intelligence*. Bantam, 2011.
24. Hendricks, Gay. *The Genius Zone*. St. Martin's Essentials, 2021.
25. Hersey, Paul, and Kenneth H. Blanchard. *Management of Organizational Behavior*. Prentice Hall, 1969.
26. "Stars." Imagine the Universe!, https://imagine.gsfc.nasa.gov/science/objects/stars1.html.
27. "Jeff Bezos Leadership Style: Traits & Skills." Vaia, https://www.-vaia.com/en-us/explanations/business-studies/business-case-studies/jeff-bezos-leadership-style/.
28. Jorgenson, Eric. *The Almanack of Naval Ravikant: A Guide to Wealth and Happiness*. HarperBusiness, 2022.
29. Knaup, Amy. "Business Employment Dynamics Data: Survival and Longevity, II." *Monthly Labor Review*, Bureau of Labor and Statistics, Sept. 2007. https://pages.stern.nyu.edu/~adamodar/pdfiles/eqnotes/survivorpaper2007.pdf
30. Keller, Gary, and Jay Papasan. *The ONE Thing*. Bard Press, 2013.
31. Koch, Richard. *The 80/20 Principle, Third Edition*. Crown Currency, 2011.
32. "NYU Stern School of Business." NYU Stern School of Business, https://stern.nyu.edu.
33. Pasricha, Neil. *The Happiness Equation*. Penguin, 2016.
34. Pendell, Ben Wigert and Ryan. "7 Problems with Your Onboarding Program." Gallup, 1 Mar. 2019, https://www.gallup.com/workplace/247172/problems-onboarding-program.aspx.
35. Robbins, Tony, and Christopher Zook. *The Holy Grail of Investing*. Simon and Schuster, 2024.
36. Sinek, Simon. *Start with Why*. Penguin, 2011.

References

37. Sinek, S. (Host). (2024, July 1). Thinking about Thinking with Brene' Brown and Adam Grant, part 2 (No. 134) [Audio podcast episode]. In A Bit of Optimism. Simon Sinek Inc. https://simonsinek.com/podcast/

38. "Situational Leadership®." Situational Leadership® Management and Leadership Training, https://situational.com/situational-leadership/?utm_source=google&utm_medium=ppc&utm_campaign=Situational%20Leadership&utm_term=situational%20leadership%20model&gad_source=1&gclid=CjoKCQjw97SzBhDaARIsAFHX-UWAjzbvJAiYH_x9_So25Su4wxksMLUNQPPTsFHoyAnon6IzI7J__t-GVYaAtoJEALw_wcB.

39. "Special Relativity." Wikipedia, https://en.wikipedia.org/wiki/Special_relativity.

40. TED: The Economics Daily. "34.7 Percent of Business Establishments Born in 2013 Were Still Operating in 2023." Bureau of Labor and Statistics, 12 Jan. 2024, https://www.bls.gov/opub/ted/2024/34-7-percent-of-business-establishments-born-in-2013-were-still-operating-in-2023.htm.

41. "The Center for Leadership Studies." Facebook, https://www.facebook.com/WeBuildLeaders/.

42. "The History of SMART Goals and OKRs." Collective Genius™ Peak Operating System for Venture Backed Companies, https://www.collective-genius.com/blog/the-history-of-smart-goals-and-okrs.

43. "The New Role of People Ops Leaders: Should HR Report to Finance or Operations?" TriNet, https://www.trinet.com/insights/who-should-hr-report-to.

44. Theil, Peter, and Blake Masters. *Zero to One*. Crown Currency, 2014.

45. "Theory of Relativity." Wikipedia, https://en.wikipedia.org/wiki/theory_of_relativity.

46. Weatherford, Jack. *Genghis Khan and the Making of the Modern World*. Crown, 2005.

47. Which Productivity Method Is Right for You?" Todoist, http://todoist.com/productivity-methods.

48. "Why Was Alexander the Great So Successful in His Conquests." DailyHistory.org, https://www.dailyhistory.org/Why_was_Alexander_the_Great_So_Successful_In_His_Conquests.